SIERRA NEVADA TREE IDENTIFIER

Sierra Nevada
TREE IDENTIFIER

by
Jim Paruk

Illustrated by Elizabeth Morales

YOSEMITE CONSERVANCY
Yosemite National Park

YOSEMITE
CONSERVANCY.

yosemiteconservancy.org

Design by Elizabeth Morales, Inverness, California

ISBN 978-0-939666-83-6

Printed in the USA by Worzalla

TABLE OF CONTENTS

DEDICATION

I dedicate this book to John Muir, who first explored, studied, and wrote about the trees of Yosemite and the Sierra Nevada. Just as Muir became graced with the spirit of these trees, may you go beyond mere identification and come to know their spirits as well.

J.P.

INTRODUCTION

The forests of the Sierra Nevada are quite diverse, playing home to about forty-five different species of trees. With elevations ranging from 2,500 to 13,000 feet, the mountain chain has a variation in climate as great as that to be experienced on a trip from California to Alaska. A rise in elevation of one vertical mile roughly corresponds with a trip one thousand miles north. This range makes the Sierra a great place to study nature and learn firsthand about the relationships that exist between climate and organisms.

One does not need training in ecology to see some basic patterns in the land. The oak woodland in the foothills has a distinctive quality, as does a sequoia forest. Each area can be recognized by its dominant vegetation. The vegetation, in turn, is affected by climate, soil, moisture, etc. Wherever similar environmental conditions exist, certain plants and animals will be found there. These areas of similar environmental conditions in the Sierra Nevada have been separated into belts based on elevation (see Appendix A). The boundary between two belts is seldom straightforward because topographic irregularities, such as canyons and peaks, influence the vegetation. Moreover, tree species in the same elevational belt on the west and east slopes may differ. Nonetheless, it is useful to know the various elevational belts as you attempt to identify trees.

Many trees grow only at particular elevations. By knowing your approximate altitude, field identification of certain trees can be greatly simplified. For example, the similar-appearing sugar and western white pines grow at different elevations (the sugar pine is lower). Also, trees often grow in association with other species. While interior live oak is found in the company of gray pine, for example, canyon live oak is not. The tree descriptions in this book provide listings of associated species to give users one more method of distinguishing trees.

Scope of This Guide

This identification manual covers forty-four native trees of the Sierra – twenty conifers (or cone-bearing trees), and twenty-four that produce flowers but not cones (broad-leaved trees). Do not be discouraged if you are unable to identify every tree – it may be a non-native species. Check Appendix B for a listing of some of the more common non-natives that are found around Sierran settlements.

Be forewarned that a tree is not always a tree. Under harsh conditions at treeline a certain tree may grow like a shrub. A shrub, under favorable conditions, may resemble and have the size of a tree.

What is a tree, then? It is defined as a woody plant with a single trunk that usually does not divide lower than ten feet off the ground. Shrubs have multiple trunks at the base and usually divide well-below ten feet from the ground. The species that fit into the large shrub/small tree category have been included.

With practice and time, you will begin to recognize the common Sierra species. You will discover that no two trees are exactly alike. Sometimes a cone or a bud may be missing, and you will have to rely on your judgement for positive identification. Every effort has been made to clear up ambiguities, but nature doesn't always fit into neat categories.

It is the goal of this book to offer practical and simple field tips for proper identification. Where space has allowed, interesting historical facts and natural history data have been provided. Good luck to you as you go about identifying and learning about the trees of the Sierra Nevada.

USING THIS BOOK

With this guide individuals with little or no experience should be able to identify the trees that inhabit the Sierra Nevada region. Long, confusing botanical terms have been omitted for the purpose of simplifying identification.

To begin, familiarize yourself with the tips below before selecting a leaf, needle, or cone as an identification specimen. Then follow this five-step procedure:

1. With your specimen for reference, turn to the "Start Here" section on page 5.

2. Choose the part of the key that appears appropriate for your specimen. (This will quickly narrow your search to a few species.)

3. Go to the page where your group is found. Is it divided into smaller sections? If so, examine your specimen and determine the section where you should begin your search.

4. Compare your specimen to the drawings in the section and read the text, paying particular attention to words or phrases in bold type, then try to make a match. Go to the page number suggested. (The entries are arranged by elevation so that the trees listed first are found at lower elevations than those at the end of the section.)

5. Read the additional text for other useful information that may aid you in positive identification. Have you found a match? If so, you have correctly identified your tree. If not, check the other species in that section before going back to Step 1.

Tips for Beginners

■ Look for differences in elevation, leaf length and

shape, silhouette, cone or seed size and shape, and habitat to distinguish similar looking species.

■ Sometimes a needle will be missing from a bundle, especially during the fall months; count several bundles to be safe.

■ Leaves on young trees are usually much larger than those on mature ones.

■ If the foliage or cones are out of reach, inspect the ground below. Keep in mind that leaves or cones from other trees might be there as well.

■ Under favorable conditions, individual trees may grow slightly above or below their elevational ranges.

■ Individual trees, like people, can depart from the norm, so consider as many characteristics as possible.

Advanced Tips

■ Pine needles come in bundles.

■ Firs have smooth, circular leaf scars and cones that sit upright.

■ Hemlocks have raised woody projections along the branches where the needles are attached.

■ Oaks have numerous terminal buds.

■ Willows have colored twigs and buds that are covered with a single scale only.

■ Cottonwoods and aspens generally have large, pointed buds.

■ Cherries and plums usually have special glands on their leaves or leafstalks, and a characteristic odor.

■ Only ashes, maples, and dogwoods have branches opposite each other.

START HERE:

■ Examine the leaves of your tree. Do they look like needles? Are the needles covered with scales? Does your tree have cones?

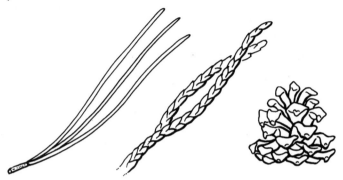

If so, go to the KEY TO CONE-BEARING TREES on page 6.

■ Alternatively, are the leaves of your tree wide and flat?

If so, go to the KEY TO BROAD-LEAVED TREES on page 12.

You're on your way to successful tree identification.

KEY: *Cone-bearing Trees*

This key is divided into three sections.
Examine the needles of your specimen.

If they are in **bundles of two or more:**

GO TO SECTION I (page 7)

If there is just a **single needle:**

GO TO SECTION II (page 9)

If the needles are **scale-like:**

GO TO SECTION III (page 11)

SECTION I:

LEAVES NEEDLE-LIKE IN CLUSTERS OF 2 OR MORE

LODGEPOLE PINE   Page 22
The only 2-needled pine in the Sierra.
Height: 20 to 80 feet. Occurrence: common
from 7,000 feet to treeline (with a few excep-
tions).

GRAY PINE   Page 24
The **8- to 12-inch-long gray-green needles**
distinguish it from ponderosa and knobcone
pines. Large cones, 6 to 10 inches long, often
remain on the uppermost branches for many
years. The trunk is usually forked or crooked.
Height: 40 to 70 feet. Occurrence: common
on west slope to 3,800 feet.

KNOBCONE PINE   Page 26
Uncommon species. The only pine with 3- to
6-inch, usually **curved cones, that grow in
whorls around the trunk and main branches
of the tree**. The 3- to 5-inch pale yellow green
needles are considerably shorter than gray
pine. Height: 20 to 45 feet. Occurrence:
known only from a few locations on the west
slope between 2,000 and 6,000 feet.

PACIFIC PONDEROSA PINE   Page 28
Bark of mature trees has distinctive puzzle-
shaped scales. Needles are 4 to 10 inches, yellow-green. Trunk is often straight. **Cones are
3 to 5 inches with projecting spines.** Similar
to Jeffrey pine; see page 117 for more detailed
comparison. Height: 60 to 180 feet.
Occurrence: abundant on west slope between
3,500 and 6,000 feet; absent from east slope.

JEFFREY PINE   Page 30
Similar to ponderosa pine, distinguished by
the size of the cones. Jeffrey has larger cones, 5
to 10 inches, that are not prickly to touch.

The **vanilla or butterscotch aroma emitted from the bark crevices** of Jeffrey can help with identification, but not always. See page 117 for a more detailed comparison. Height: 80 to 130 feet. Occurrence: found on both slopes from 6,000 feet to treeline.

SUGAR PINE   Page 23
Similar to western white pine but taller, up to 220 feet, with longer cones (10 to 16 inches) and **long horizontal branches**. Bark is divided into long, vertical ridges and furrows. Generally found at lower elevations than western white pine (see page 34 for a more detailed comparison). Occurrence: common on west slope from 4,000 to 7,500 feet.

WESTERN WHITE PINE   Page 34
Similar to sugar pine but smaller, 80 to 120 feet, with smaller cones (5 to 9 inches) and **top branches that extend upward**. Mature bark divided into squarish or rectangular plates. Occurrence: locally common from 7,000 feet to near treeline.

FOXTAIL PINE   Page 36
The **only 5-needled pine with short needles consistently less than 1.5 inches long,** bunched together like a bottle brush along the branches. Reddish-cones are 3 to 5 inches. Height: 20 to 50 feet. Occurrence: **often in pure stands** on both slopes, from Sequoia and Kings Canyon National Park south, between 9,000 and 11,500 feet.

LIMBER PINE   Page 38
Similar to whitebark pine. Both are high-altitude pines with flexible twigs and yellow-green needles, 2 to 3 inches long. **Cones** are 4 to 5 inches, turning **green to brown** during the season. If cones are not visible, look beneath the tree. Height: 40 to 50 feet. Occurrence: uncommon on both slopes, from Mono Pass in Yosemite Park south, between 8,000 and 12,000 feet.

WHITEBARK PINE   Page 40
Similar to limber pine. Often appears in
dense, shrub-like clusters at treeline. **Cones
are purple**, 2 to 3 inches long. Height: up to
35 feet. Occurrence: common on both slopes
from 8,500 feet to treeline.

SECTION II:

SINGLE NEEDLE-LIKE LEAVES

A. NEEDLES IN HORIZONTAL ROWS, OR ASCENDING

CALIFORNIA NUTMEG   Page 42
Needles glossy, flat, 1 to 2 inches, with **sharp
tips; aromatic when crushed. Fruits fleshy,
olive-like**. Height: 20 to 50 feet.
Occurrence: sporadic on west slope, on moist
slopes in river canyons between 2,000 and
6,000 feet.

PACIFIC YEW   Page 44
Needles 0.5 to 1 inch, soft and odorless. Bark
smooth and peeling. **Fruit** is a **distinctive
bright, red berry**. Height: shrub or small tree
up to 35 feet. Occurrence: prefers growing
beneath a forest canopy on the west slope
mostly north of Yosemite, up to 7,000 feet.

WHITE FIR   Page 46
Needles **usually with a one-quarter twist at
base**, pale blue-green, 0.75 to 2 inches,
distinctly 2-sided, not easily rolled between
fingers. Typically, needles grow in flat sprays
or horizontal to the branches, but will occasionally be erect. Bark yellow-brown on
inside. Height: 70 to 180 feet tall.
Occurrence: common on west slope between
3,500 and 7,000 feet, and on east slope from
7,500 to 8,500 feet.

CALIFORNIA RED FIR
Page 48

Needles lacking one-quarter twist at base, dark bluegreen, 0.75 to 1 inch, mostly curved, 4-sided, usually densely crowded toward and on top of branches; can be twirled between fingers. Needles mostly erect (especially on young trees), but will be in horizontal rows on occasion. **Deep red inner bark is distinctive.** Height: 60 to 160 feet. Occurrence: abundant on west slope between 6,000 and 9,000 feet, and on east slope from 8,000 to 9,500 feet.

B. NEEDLES GROWING OUT IN ALL DIRECTIONS FROM THE BRANCHES

DOUGLAS-FIR
Page 50

Similar to firs and nutmeg. Cones of Douglas-fir hang down, those of other firs sit upright. The long, pointed projections between the scales of the Douglas-fir cone are distinctive. In the absence of cones, examine the "growing tips." **Firs have small, blunt buds, those of Douglas-fir will be long and pointed.** Height: to 180 feet. Occurrence: locally common on west slope from Mariposa County north between 3,500 and 5,500 feet.

MOUNTAIN HEMLOCK
Page 52

Drooping top is characteristic. Raised, peg-like projections at the base of needles are distinctive. Height: to 100 feet. Occurrence: found on both slopes, mostly in north-facing bowls, from 8,000 feet to treeline.

SINGLELEAF PINYON PINE
Page 54

Needles are curved, 1.5 to 2 inches, **stiff and rounded. Papery sheath at base of each needle is diagnostic.** Small tree up to 30 feet tall. Occurrence: abundant on east slope from 5,000 to 7,500 feet, rare on west slope.

SECTION III:

LEAVES TINY, SCALE-LIKE

INCENSE CEDAR   Page 56
Leaves are bright green, soft and smooth, **aromatic when crushed**; ends of **branches look like they have been ironed flat**. Height: 60 to 150 feet. Occurrence: common on west slope between 3,500 and 7,000 feet.

GIANT SEQUOIA   Page 58
Large rare tree, **leaves** are dark green, prickly to touch and **not aromatic**; ends of branches are three dimensional, not flat. Height: to 250 feet. Occurrence: uncommon in scattered groves on west slope between 5,000 and 8,000 feet.

WESTERN JUNIPER   Page 60
Leaves are bright to bluish green, **usually covered with white resin**; end of branches are thick and rounded. **Fleshy, berry-like fruit is distinctive**. Height: 15 to 50 feet. Occurrence: found on both slopes between 7,000 and 9,000 feet.

KEY: *Broad-leaved Trees*

This key is divided into four sections. Examine the leaves of your tree. Determine if they are compound or simple.

Compound leaves are composed of three or more small leaflets. They can either be attached in rows to the central stalk (pinnate) or from the end of the leafstalk, like fingers spreading from a hand (palmate).

Simple leaves are made up of a single leaf. To decide which section to use look at the leaf and determine if it has lobed, toothed, or untoothed edges. WARNING: Some trees that produce leaves that are usually toothed will occasionally show untoothed leaves. You might have to check both sections before you arrive at the correct answer. Certain species that are easily confused are listed in both sections.

1. If they are **compound:**

GO TO SECTION 1 (page 14)

Pinnate  Palmate

2. If they are **lobed simple leaves:**

GO TO SECTION 2 (page 15)

Lobed simple leaves are leaves that are shallowly or deeply cut into narrow or broad lobes.

3. If they are **toothed simple leaves:**

GO TO SECTION 3 (page 16)

Toothed simple leaves are leaves without lobes and with edges that are serrated, like the blade of a saw. Teeth can be of uniform size, as in willows, or of alternating size, as in alders. Some species, such as cottonwoods, have blunt or wavy leaf edges.

4. If they are **untoothed simple leaves:**

GO TO SECTION 4 (page 20)

Untoothed simple leaves are smooth-edged leaves without teeth or lobes.

SECTION 1:

COMPOUND LEAVES

SIERRA BLADDERNUT Page 62
Uncommon. Leaves 2 to 5 inches, made up of 3 oval to nearly circular leaflets, each between 1 and 2.5 inches, with margins finely toothed. Height: shrub or small tree to 15 feet. Occurrence: sporadic on west slope to 4,500 feet.

CALIFORNIA BUCKEYE Page 64
Leaves are palmate, made up of 7 leaflets (occasionally 5), 3 to 7 inches. Height: often shrub-like, to 25 feet. Fruit is 2 to 3 inches, resembling a pear. The tree drops its leaves in mid-summer. Occurrence: common on west slope up to 3,500 feet.

OREGON ASH Page 66
Leaves pinnate, 5 to 12 inches, with 5 to 7 leaflets, each 2 to 5 inches long. Notice that the leaves grow opposite each other, unlike those of black walnut. **Fruit is distinctive, resembling light brown miniature canoe paddles that hang in dense clusters**. Height: to 60 feet. Occurrence: common on west slope in canyons and along streamsides up to 5,000 feet.

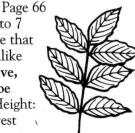

CALIFORNIA ASH Page 66
Similar to Oregon ash. Leaves of California ash are smaller, 3 to 6 inches, and leaflets more sharply toothed. **Twigs are also distinctive, being 4-sided**, compared to the rounded twigs of Oregon ash. Height: to 15 feet. Occurrence: uncommon along streams of the western slope up to 3,500 feet.

SECTION 2:

LOBED SIMPLE LEAVES

WESTERN SYCAMORE   Page 68
The most **distinctive feature is the whitish,
smooth, peeling bark**. Leaves are deeply
lobed, nearly halfway to center, into 5 sections
(sometimes 3) that resemble a star. **Fruit
consists of 2 to 7 balls, nearly an inch wide,
that hang down on a long stalk**. Height: 40
to 80 feet. Occurrence: common along
streams and canyons on west slope up to 3,000
feet.

BLUE OAK   Page 70
The small (1 to 3 inch) blue-green shallowly-
lobed leaves are seldom confused with those of
any other species. **Twigs are hairy**. Height:
to 60 feet. Occurrence: common on west
slope to 3,000 feet.

VALLEY OAK   Page 72
Small leaves for such a large tree are dull
green, 2 to 4 inches, with 7 to 11 deep lobes.
Twigs are not hairy. Height: to 100 feet.
Occurrence: restricted to foothills of western
slope mostly below 3,000 feet.

CALIFORNIA BLACK OAK   Page 74
**No other oak in the Sierra has deeply lobed
leaves with bristle-tipped edges**. Leaves are
larger (4 to 7 inches) than those of valley oak.
Height: to 80 feet. Occurrence: common
on west slope throughout the Sierra up to
7,000 feet.

BIG-LEAF MAPLE   Page 76
Foliage of this tree is unique in the Sierra.
Large leaves, 6 to 10 inches long and wide,
grow opposite each other. Height: small to
large tree to 70 feet. Occurrence: common
on west slope to 5,500 feet.

SECTION 3:

TOOTHED SIMPLE LEAVES

A. SMALL LEAVES, MOSTLY LESS THAN 1.5 INCHES LONG

BIRCH-LEAF MOUNTAIN-
MAHOGANY   Page 78
Leaves are broadest beyond the middle (see
drawing) and finely toothed; their undersurface
is usually covered with velvety hairs. Fruit is
slim, with a twisted tail covered with white
hairs. Height: more shrub-like, can reach 20
feet. Occurrence: common on west slope up
to 6,000 feet.

B. LEAVES THICK AND WAXY, HOLLY-LIKE. Usually two types of leaves on the same tree. May have spiny-tipped or smooth edges.

INTERIOR LIVE OAK   Page 80
Resembles canyon live oak. **Undersurface of
leaves hairless**; acorns usually less than 0.5
inch with no yellow fuzz. Height: 30 to 70
feet. Occurrence: common on west slope up to
4,000 feet.

CANYON LIVE OAK   Page 82
Similar to interior live oak. Undersurface of
leaves hairy; **acorns** usually larger than 0.5
inch, **covered in yellow fuzz**. Height: 20 to
80 feet. Occurrence: common on west slope
below 6,500 feet.

C. LONG, LINEAR LEAVES FOUR TIMES LONGER THAN WIDE, WITH BRIGHT RED OR YELLOW TWIGS, AND NARROW CLUSTER OF CATKINS OR "PUSSY WILLOWS."

Leaves may not always have well-developed toothed margins. Common along streams and rivercourses.

SHINING WILLOW   Page 85
Can be identified by glandular leaf stalks (look for **2 or more black spots on the stem** that support the leaf). Leaves are dark green above and paler beneath. Height: to 50 feet. Occurrence: common to 8,000 feet on both slopes of the Sierra.

RED WILLOW   Page 85
Leaves are **lighter green above** than shining willow and lack the glandular leaf stalks. Height: to 50 feet. Occurrence: along streams of west slope below 5,000 feet.

GOODDING'S BLACK WILLOW   Page 84
Unlike the two species above, this willow's leaves **are the same shade of gray-green on both surfaces.** Its **yellowish twigs can be snapped neatly off.** Height: to 35 feet. Occurrence: on west slope mostly below 2,000 feet.

D. THE REMAINDER OF THE TOOTHED SPECIES are listed starting with those having long, linear leaves followed by those with successively wider leaves. Match the leaf with the drawing and read the description for positive identification.

PACIFIC MADRONE
See Section 4B (page 20)

BITTER CHERRY   Page 86
Leaves 1 to 3 inches long, with shallow serrated
edges, often with 1 or 2 small glands at the base
of the leaf. **Bark is smooth, silvery to red-
brown, with horizontal streaks.** Fruit is a red
to black berry. Height: to 15 feet. Occurrence:
common on west slope, 4,000 to 8,000 feet.

BLACK COTTONWOOD   Page 88
Leaves 3 to 6 inches long, 2 to 4 inches wide,
shiny dark green above, paler beneath.
Leafstalks are rounded and easily rolled
between fingers. **End buds are larger** (greater
than 1/2 inch) than those of any other poplar
in Sierra. Height: 30 to 120 feet. Occurrence:
common on west slope along streams to 6,000
feet, with individuals to 9,000 feet, and east
slope to 7,000 feet.

CASCARA   Page 90
Leaves 3 to 6 inches **with 10 to 15 prominent
pairs of parallel veins** that run to finely
toothed edges. Fruit is a black berry. Height:
shrub to 25 feet. Occurrence: sporadic on west
slope in moist places mostly from Yosemite
north.

WHITE ALDER   Page 92
Leaves 2 to 3.5 inches long, about half as wide,
serrated edges prominent, with 9 to 12 parallel
veins visible on the undersurface of the leaf.
Look for drooping cones, about 0.5 inch long.
Height: 35 to 70 feet. Occurrence: common
along watercourses on west slope mostly below
5,000 feet.

WESTERN CHOKE-CHERRY   Page 94
Leaves 2 to 5 inches long, about half as wide,
and sharply serrated with pointed tip. Often
with 1 or 2 small glands at the base of the leafstalk. Fruit is a purple berry. Height: shrub to
20 feet. Occurrence: common in moist places
from 1,500 to 7,000 feet.

WATER BIRCH   Page 96
Smooth, red to brownish bark with white, horizontal lines. Leaves are 1 to 2 inches long, about half (or more) as wide; serrations are present except at base of leaf. Height: shrub-like, can reach 25 feet. Occurrence: found along watercourses on both slopes below 8,000 feet.

SIERRA PLUM   Page 98
Leaves 1 to 3 inches long, nearly round, sharply serrated, with glands present at base occasionally. Fruit is a red plum, about an inch long. Height: shrub to 20 feet. Occurrence: on west slope, mostly south of Yosemite, near streams between 4,000 and 6,000 feet.

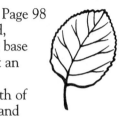

FREMONT COTTONWOOD   Page 100
Triangular leaves, 2 to 3 inches, yellow-green on both surfaces (unlike black cottonwood which is dark green above, paler beneath), with flattened leafstalks not easily rolled between the fingers. Height: 40 to 80 feet. Occurrence: locally common on **west slope** along watercourses **below 2,500 feet**, and on **east slope mostly below 5,000 feet**, with individuals to 6,500 feet.

QUAKING ASPEN   Page 102
Leaves are nearly round, 1.5 to 3 inches, with finely serrated leaf edges. Bark is white and smooth becoming fissured with age. Height: 10 to 65 feet. Occurrence: common on both sides of the Sierra, usually near water or on moist slopes **between 6,000 and 10,000 feet.**

SECTION 4:

UNTOOTHED SIMPLE LEAVES

A. LEAVES NEARLY AS WIDE AS LONG

WESTERN REDBUD   Page 104
**No other Sierran tree has the distinctive
heart-shaped leaves, 2 to 3.5 inches.** Notice
the 7 to 9 veins that connect to the notched
base. Exhibits brown or purplish pea pods and
beautiful red-purple buds which open in early
spring. Height: more shrub-like, can reach 20
feet. Occurrence: common on west slope up
to 3,500 feet.

MOUNTAIN DOGWOOD   Page 106
Leaves are 2 1/2 to 4 1/2 inches, **with 5 to 6
long, curving veins on each side of the center
that run laterally to the tip.** Height: short
tree, 20 to 50 feet. Occurrence: common on
west slope between 2,500 and 6,000 feet.

B. LEAVES LONGER THAN WIDE

INTERIOR LIVE OAK
See Section 3B (page 16)

CANYON LIVE OAK
See Section 3B (page 16)

PACIFIC MADRONE   Page 108
Smooth, reddish bark on trunk and limbs.
The thin outer bark is easily peeled away
revealing a gray or yellow inner layer. **Leaves
are thick and leathery,** 4 to 6 inches long and
1 to 3 inches wide, occasionally with toothed
margins. Fruit is berry-like. Height: to 50
feet. Occurrence: mostly north of Yosemite on
west slope below 5,000 feet.

CALIFORNIA BAY   Page 110
Thick, **leathery leaves**, 2 to 5 inches. Shiny
dark green above, paler beneath, **aromatic
when crushed**. Evergreen. Height: medium-
sized tree, 40 to 80 feet. Occurrence: common
on west slope to 5,500 feet.

SCOULER'S WILLOW   Page 84
Leaves vary in size, with consistently wider
middle section. Dark green above, usually hairy
beneath. **Twigs give off skunk-like odor when
rubbed.** Height: usually a shrub, can reach 15
feet. Occurrence: found on both slopes up to
11,000 feet.

ARROYO WILLOW   Page 84
Can be distinguished from other willows by its
light-colored bark with white blotches.
Height: to 25 feet. Occurrence: found along
streamsides up to 7,000 feet.

CURL-LEAF MOUNTAIN-
MAHOGANY   Page 112
The only shrub or tree in the Sierra **with small
(0.5 to 1.5 inches) leaves with margins curled
under**. Evergreen. Height: usually less than
15 feet. Occurrence: **abundant on east side of
Sierra** from 5,000 feet to near treeline, sporadic
on west slope.

Lodgepole Pine

Pinus contorta ssp. murrayana

HABITAT & RANGE

Usually forms extensive pure stands at high elevations on both slopes of the Sierra, from 7,000 to 10,000 feet, but may occur above and below this zone. For example, it is sparsely scattered along water courses down to 4,000 feet in Yosemite Valley.

INFORMATION

Throughout much of its range, lodgepole is regarded as a fire dependent species; normally seeds are released only when the resin that holds the cones tightly together has been melted by fire. In the Sierra, however, cones will open (usually in August or September) whether there is fire or not. Solar radiation heats the resin above 113° F, its melting point, and the seeds are freed. Chickarees, chipmunks, crossbills, and nutcrackers feed on the abundant seed crop.

Lodgepole is unique among conifers as it can successfully reproduce as early as six years of age. Seeds from young trees are just as viable as those from older and more mature individuals. Young lodgepoles often grow in extremely dense stands, eventually crowding themselves out as the entire group becomes stagnant. This tendency towards overcrowding is probably the most extreme of any tree in North America.

Some lodgepole forests appear to be dead or dying, usually as a result of needleminer moth infestation, although recent drought conditions have been hard on these trees. A major needleminer outbreak occurred during the 1960s and killed many trees. The larvae of the insect live inside and feed on the pine needles. Lodgepoles can tolerate a high degree of infestation without suffering any serious side effects.

DESCRIPTION
- **Size:** medium-sized tree, 20 to 70 feet (6-21 m)
- **Shape:** tall and slender with narrow crown
- **Bark:** grayish, thin, and scaly; bark scales with yellow edge
- **Needles:** in 2's, 1.25 to 3 inches (3-6 cm), usually with a slight twist, yellow-green to dark green
- **Cones:** egg-shaped, 0.75 to 2 inches (3-5 cm), stalkless, with prickles (some remain closed on tree for many years)

SIMILAR SPECIES
None. No other Sierran conifer has two needles per bundle.

ASSOCIATED SPECIES
Whitebark pine, mountain hemlock, western juniper, and California red fir can be found interspersed in large lodgepole stands, typically above 8,500 feet.

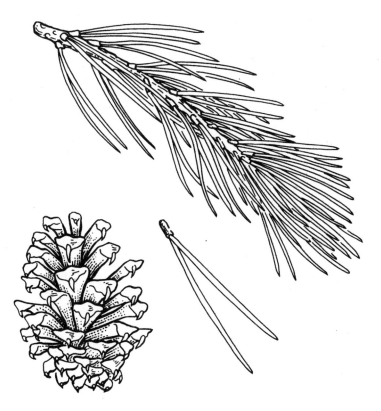

Gray Pine

Bull Pine, Digger Pine
Pinus sabiniana

HABITAT & RANGE

Common on dry western slopes and ridges in foothills and low mountains up to 3,000 feet, and uncommon up to 6,000 feet. Not found in the foothills west of Sequoia and Kings Canyon National Parks.

INFORMATION

This pine has long, sparsely-growing needles, an attribute that led early pioneers to describe it as "the tree that you can see through." As a result, it offers little shade in areas where it would be welcomed. While it usually grows vertically on a hillside, the gray pine will grow at a right angle, away from the slope. This trait separates it from other Sierran trees. In addition, its large cones, second only to those of the Coulter pine in size and weight, make the gray pine easy to identify from a distance.

Cones mature by early fall of their second year and remain on the branches for several years. Woodpeckers, jays and other foothill birds, as well as squirrels and chipmunks consume the seeds. The sweet seeds were also gathered and eaten by Southern Miwok people.

With its pale foliage and deep roots, gray pine is well-adapted to living in the harsh Sierran foothill environment. Because it can grow on rocky outcrops and in thin, poor soils (like serpentine) unsuitable for other foothill trees, it inhabits some unlikely and inhospitable places.

SIMILAR SPECIES

Knobcone pine. Notice the small, tightly-closed cones of the knobcone compared to the large and open cones of the gray pine.

DESCRIPTION
- **Size:** medium-sized tree, 40 to 70 feet (12-21 m)
- **Shape:** sparse gray foliage reveals a forked trunk, large cones, and upsweeping branches
- **Bark:** gray to brown, becoming furrowed with age and revealing bright orange underbark
- **Needles:** 3 to a bundle, 8 to 12 inches (20-30 cm), gray-green, with many white lines that droop from the ends of the twigs
- **Cones:** large, 6 to 10 inches (15-25 cm) long and 5 to 9 inches (11-23 cm) wide, egg-shaped. After opening, may remain on the upper branches of the tree for several years.

ASSOCIATED SPECIES
Knobcone pine, interior live oak, blue oak.

Knobcone Pine

Pinus attenuata

HABITAT & RANGE
A rare pine on the western slope, mostly below 4,000 feet from Mariposa county north.

INFORMATION
This little-known pine is seldom seen and a challenge to find. It grows above Arch Rock Entrance Station (along Highway 140) at Yosemite National Park, and on selected ridges within the Sierra National Forest.

No other tree hoards its own cones like the knobcone. The cones grow rigidly attached to the branches and trunk (not at the ends of branches as with other pines), typically in pairs or circles of three to five cones. On rare occasions, as many as seventeen cones have been found encircling a trunk. The knobcone has been called "the tree that swallows its own cones," for the way its trunk engulfs cones with its expanding wood.

Knobcones depend on fire for survival; sufficient heat is needed to open cones and release seeds, and fire is required to prepare a suitable seed bed. Between fires, the cones may remain on the tree for as long as thirty years. After a fire, the seedlings sprout vigorously, and like lodgepoles, will produce cones when only five or six years old.

SIMILAR SPECIES
Gray pine. Knobcones will occasionally have a forked trunk similar to the gray pine, so the best distinguishing feature is cone size. Gray pines have large cones usually found on the uppermost branches, while knobcone pines have smaller ones that grow all along the branches and trunk.

ASSOCIATED SPECIES
Gray pine, interior live oak, and blue oak.

DESCRIPTION

- **Size:** small tree, 20 to 30 feet (6-9 m)
- **Bark:** dull gray-brown, shallowly furrowed
- **Needles:** in 3's, 3 to 5 inches (7-12.5 cm), pale yellow green
- **Cones:** curved, asymmetrical, 3 to 6 inches (7-15 cm), usually buried in pairs or circles beneath the expanding bark of branches and trunk; they remain closed on the tree for many years
- **Shape:** variable, but usually having many clusters of small cones

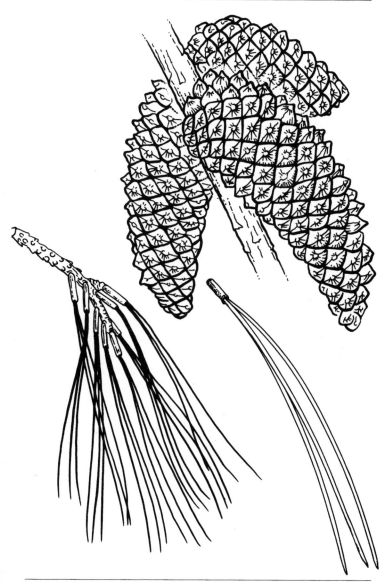

Pacific Ponderosa Pine

Western Yellow Pine
Pinus ponderosa

HABITAT & RANGE
Common throughout the Sierra on the west slope up to 7,000 feet. It can tolerate a range of growing conditions, from moist to dry ground, from tops of ridges to canyon bottoms.

INFORMATION
The Pacific ponderosa pine is the most widely distributed of North American pines, growing from southern Canada to northern Mexico. It grows under a variety of environmental conditions with differing soil types, pH levels, and moisture contents.

By sending down fast-growing roots, the ponderosa can out-compete other trees on more exposed slopes. A seedling just 3 inches tall may have a taproot 24 inches long. Moreover, seedlings can withstand prolonged drought that would kill other trees. These and other survival adaptations make the ponderosa pine a genuinely hardy tree.

The bark of 300- to 600-year-old trees is very thick and often covered with fire scars. Scientists have found trees they believe to have survived over 20 fires. Unusually hot forest fires can be deadly for the species, however. Exceptionally large ponderosas succumbed to the raging fires that swept through Yosemite in August, 1990.

Ponderosa reproduction throughout its range is irregular; it appears that good seed production occurs in areas with above average rainfall.

SIMILAR SPECIES
See pg. 117 for comparison with Jeffrey pine.

DESCRIPTION
- **Size:** large tree, 60 to 180 feet (18-60 m)
- **Shape:** crowns of young- to medium-aged trees are slender and spine-like; crowns of mature trees are flattened with main branches sweeping downward only to ascend abruptly at their ends
- **Bark:** on mature trees, furrowed and breaks off into distinct puzzle-shaped pieces, outer bark is tan, inner bark is sulphur-yellow; on young trees bark is not furrowed and does not form puzzle-shaped scales, outer bark is brown to black
- **Needles:** in 3's, (not uncommon to find 4), 4 to 8 inches (10-20 cm), glossy, from yellow to dark green
- **Cones:** 2 to 5 inches (5-12 cm), tips of scales sharp, prickly to touch

ASSOCIATED SPECIES
Several, see pg. 114 under "Ponderosa Pine/Mixed Coniferous Belt."

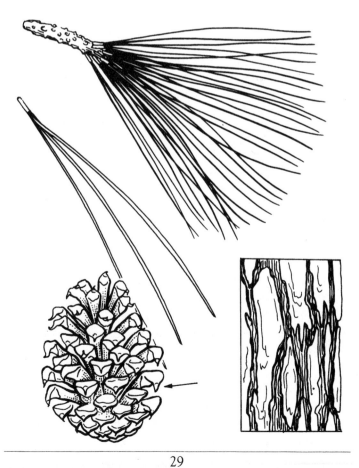

Jeffrey Pine

Pinus jeffreyi

HABITAT & RANGE
Common on the west slope starting at 5,200 feet in the north, and 6,000 feet in the central and south, disappearing at about 9,000 feet. It is more abundant on the east slope between 6,000 and 9,500 feet.

INFORMATION
At first glance, Jeffrey and Pacific ponderosa pines seem very similar and easy to confuse, but there are reliable ways to tell them apart. The color of the inner surface of the scales that make up the bark is a characteristic that can help make such identification easier. For detailed information on distinguishing these two species, see page 117.

The Jeffrey pine is apparently more resistant to frost during the seedling stage than is the ponderosa. This may help explain why Jeffrey is more prevalent along meadows below ridges (which serve as cold-air sinks), more commonly known as "frost pockets."

Seed crops are produced at irregular intervals of four to eight years. The seeds, which are twice the size of the ponderosa's, are eaten by rodents. Jeffrey pines live for four to five hundred years.

SIMILAR SPECIES
Ponderosa pine (see page 28).

ASSOCIATED SPECIES
On the west slope, California red fir, occasional white fir, and Pacific ponderosa pine. On the east slope, singleleaf pinyon pine, curl-leaf mountain-mahogany, and California red fir.

DESCRIPTION

■ **Size:** medium to large tree, 80 to 130 feet (24-39 m)
■ **Bark:** reddish brown, deeply furrowed, with distinct puzzle-shaped scales on outside of some trees
■ **Needles:** 3 in a bundle, 5 to 10 inches (13-25 cm), gray-green to blue-green, stiff, and pointed
■ **Cones:** oval, 5 to 8 inches (13-20 cm), widest at base, with pointy tips that usually curve inward

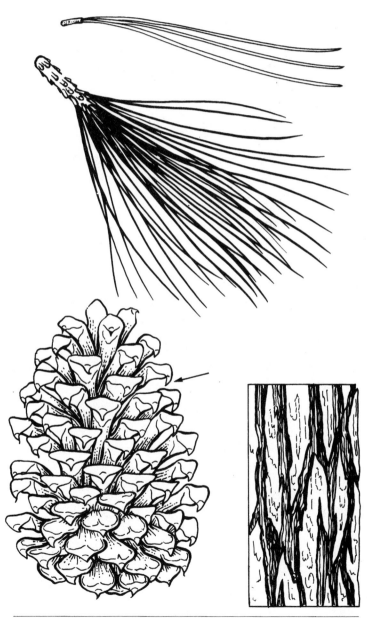

Sugar Pine

Pinus lambertiana

HABITAT & RANGE

Common on dry western slopes in mixed coniferous forests throughout the Sierra from 3,500 to 7,500 feet, occasionally higher.

INFORMATION

Few trees are more inspiring than the sugar pine, the world's tallest pine (over 220 feet) with the world's longest cone (the record is 28 inches). And unlike most conifers with conventional growth forms, no two sugar pines are exactly alike.

The tree does not produce cones regularly or in great abundance, but good crops will occur at intervals of four to six years, most cones being produced by the dominant trees in the area. Chickarees cut down as many as half of them before they mature, and white-headed woodpeckers may riddle another third. Sugar pine beetles (*Conophthorus lamerinaiae*) are responsible for destroying many more. It is a wonder that there are any large seeds left to germinate.

At lower and middle elevations sugar pine grows best on north and east facing slopes, preferring areas that receive at least twenty inches of precipitation annually. The healthiest stands are found in the elevation belt between 4,500 and 6,000 feet.

Any wounds to the tree cause it to produce a thick resin that oozes into the injured area, then solidifies into white nodules sweet with pine sugar (a substance from which the tree drew its name).

SIMILAR SPECIES

Western white pine, see pg. 34 for discussion.

ASSOCIATED SPECIES

Several, see pg. 114 under "Ponderosa Pine/Mixed Coniferous Belt."

DESCRIPTION

- **Size:** large tree, 100 to 240 feet (30-75 m)
- **Shape:** a broad, open crown
- **Bark:** dark red or purple, narrowly furrowed forming irregular-shaped scales which break off easily
- **Needles:** in 5's, slender, 2.75 to 4 inches (7-19 cm), covered with white lines
- **Cones:** 11 to 18 inches (26-46 cm), frequently hanging from the tips of branches
- **Other:** large horizontal branches spread at an angle nearly perpendicular to the trunk

Western White Pine

Silver Pine
Pinus monticola

HABITAT & RANGE

On the west slope in dry habitats mostly between 7,500 and 10,500 feet; locally prevalent on the east slope from the Mammoth Lakes area south. It is never abundant except in local stands.

INFORMATION

In comparison with other pines, the western white bears few cones. Only forty to fifty cones are the normal output of a typical tree. Cones are borne at irregular intervals, generally every three to four years. The seeds are eaten by chipmunks and squirrels.

An important timber tree in some areas, western white pine is used mostly today in the manufacture of wooden matches. White pine blister rust (a fungus accidentally introduced from Europe around 1900) is deadly to this pine. It forms a yellow blister then white sacs on the tree's twigs. The fungus has spread and destroyed millions of native trees which can offer no natural defense to this foreign invader.

SIMILAR SPECIES

Sugar and western white pines share many similar characteristics (as does whitebark pine). Knowing your elevation is one reliable way to distinguish them. Sugar pine grows at the lowest elevations (3,500-6,500 feet north and 4,500-8,000 feet south). Then comes western white (5,500-8,000 feet north, 8,000-11,000 feet south) and whitebark (3,500-9,500 feet north, 9,500-11,000 feet south).

DESCRIPTION
- **Size:** large tree, 100 to 150 feet (30-40 m)
- **Shape:** slender crown when growing in thick stands, but is more open and spreading growing in exposed areas
- **Bark:** light gray on young trees becoming divided into squarish or rectangular brownish-orange sections with age
- **Needles:** in 5's, 2 to 4 inches (5-10 cm), blue-green, tips with short, blunt points
- **Cones:** narrow, yellow-brown, 5 to 9 inches (13-23 cm), with a prominent stalk

ASSOCIATED SPECIES
California red fir, Jeffrey and lodgepole pines, and western juniper.

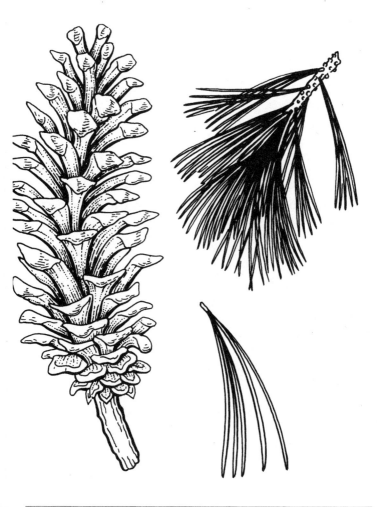

Foxtail Pine

Pinus balfouriana

HABITAT & RANGE
It grows south of Yosemite in scattered stands on dry, exposed, rocky ridges on both slopes between 9,000 and 12,000 feet.

INFORMATION
Foxtail pines grow in high areas where bitter winds, cold temperatures and poor soils are the norm. These hardy trees survive because they have made adaptations which include deep spreading roots, long-lived needles, and the ability to prosper without bark (up to 90% can be lost).

Because the soils in which they grow are often coarse and well-drained, foxtails have developed roots that more closely resemble those of a cactus than those of the typical Sierran tree. To conserve energy during drought-like summer conditions, they keep their needles longer than most other pines. Instead of shedding them every few years, foxtails retain them for up to seventeen years.

The tree takes its name from the appearance of the densely-clothed needles that surround its branches. They are said to resemble the hairs that make up a fox's tail. Little is known about the tree's longevity, but some feel it can live up to 500 years or longer. The foxtail pine was more common in earlier geologic time than it is today.

SIMILAR SPECIES
None. Although limber and whitebark pines grow at similar elevations and have needles in groups of five, their needle length is considerably longer than that of the foxtail.

ASSOCIATED SPECIES
Whitebark and lodgepole pines, mountain hemlock.

DESCRIPTION

■ **Size:** small to medium sized tree, 20 to 50 feet (6-15 m); a shrub at timberline

■ **Shape:** usually upright with slender crown

■ **Bark:** whitish-gray and smooth, becoming darker and furrowed with age

■ **Needles:** 5 to a bundle, short, only 1 to 1.25 inches (2-4 cm), with sharp tips, densely covering the twigs and much of the branches

■ **Cones:** 3.5 to 5 inches (9-13 cm), cylindrical, reddish-brown with tapered bases

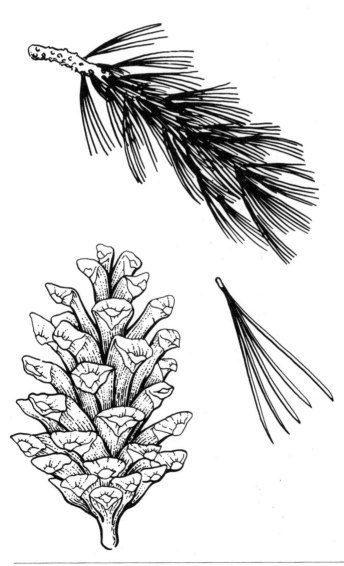

Limber Pine

Pinus flexilis

HABITAT & RANGE

An uncommon tree because of its limited range in the Sierra. It grows only on the east slope between 8,000 and 12,000 feet from Mono Pass in Yosemite National Park south.

INFORMATION

Named for its extremely flexible twigs, the limber pine grows in windy areas too harsh for most other tree species. Its twigs are filled with oily balsam and can be tied into overhand knots without breaking. This characteristic alone is not a good field identifier as the whitebark pine features similar twigs.

The limber pine exhibits peculiar growth habits. Branches on young trees grow horizontally in whorls before angling toward the ground. Older trees may have long limbs (12 to 18 feet) out of proportion to their trunks that eventually curve downward. Also distinctive of limber is the dense growth of needles at the end of its branches. Little is known about the longevity of the limber pine, but it is doubtful that individuals live beyond 300 years.

Birds and mammals, especially Clark's nutcrackers and squirrels, consume the seeds. Nutcrackers will cache the seeds in hundreds of spots, most of which are re-located when they return ten months later.

SIMILAR SPECIES

Whitebark pine. The best distinguishing characteristic is the cone. Whitebark has smaller, purple cones while those of the limber are brown and somewhat longer. The species are difficult to tell apart without cones being present.

ASSOCIATED SPECIES

Whitebark and lodgepole pines.

DESCRIPTION

- **Size:** short tree, 35 to 50 feet (11-15 m)
- **Shape:** often short and squatty, with limbs that grow erect or horizontally
- **Bark:** young bark whitish and smooth; old bark is brown or black and scaly
- **Needles:** 5 to a bundle, 2 to 3.5 inches (5-9 cm), slender, light or dark green, with white lines present on all surfaces
- **Cones:** 3 to 6 inches (7.5-15 cm), oval, light brown, with short stalks; tips of scales rounded

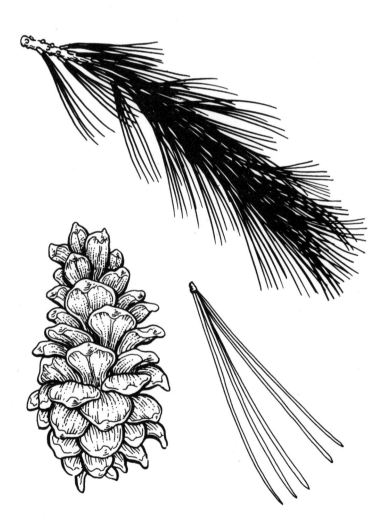

Whitebark Pine

Pinus albicaulis

HABITAT & RANGE

Common on dry, rocky soils on both sides of the Sierra from as low as 7,500 feet in the north to 12,000 feet in the south.

INFORMATION

Whitebarks are associated with timberline, the highest elevation where trees will grow. This is likely the last tree species hikers will encounter in crossing a Sierran summit or pass. Whitebarks must cope with harsh environmental conditions such as strong and persistent winds, cold winter temperatures, and short growing seasons.

Winds cause the tree (as well as other vegetation near timberline) to assume a prostrate, shrubby form. Botanists call any tree that is pruned or shaped by the wind *krummholz* (the German word for crooked wood).

Whitebarks grow very slowly, some taking as long as 500 years to grow to be seven inches in diameter. Needles may remain on the trees for up to eight years. Cones mature in late August or early September of their second year. Some cones may never open, their seeds eventually rotting. Those that do open in late autumn drop their seeds to the ground beneath the parent tree.

Clark's nutcrackers come annually to open the cones and extract the seeds, which are either eaten or stored. Oddly, some of the seeds are never retrieved from their underground caches. In this way, Clark's nutcrackers have been instrumental in establishing new colonies of whitebark pine.

SIMILAR SPECIES

Limber pine. Contrast the purple cones of the whitebark with the brown cones of the limber. See the limber pine description (page 38) for additional ways to distinguish these two species.

DESCRIPTION
- **Size:** small tree, 3 to 35 feet (1-10.5 m), frequently shrubby at higher elevations
- **Shape:** below timberline erect, but above timberline often assumes shrubby and prostrate appearance with a gnarled or twisted trunk
- **Bark:** thin, smooth, mostly white on the surface, reddish brown on the inside
- **Needles:** 5 in a bundle, 1 1/2 to 2 3/4 inches (4-7 cm), crowded at the ends of twigs; foliage has sweet to pungent taste and odor.
- **Cones:** purple, 1 1/2 to 3 1/4 inches (3-7 cm), remaining closed at maturity.

ASSOCIATED SPECIES
Foxtail, limber and lodgepole pines, mountain hemlock.

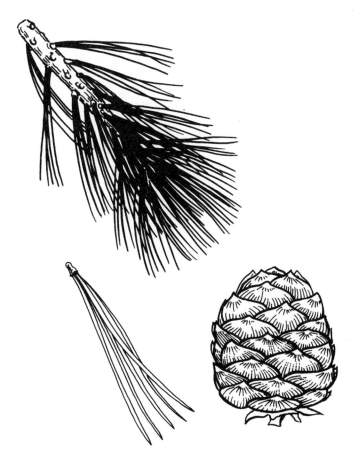

California Nutmeg

California Torreya, Stinking-cedar
Torreya californica

HABITAT & RANGE
Uncommon, preferring moist, shaded, north-facing slopes (but found in open, sunny, exposed locations), usually near watercourses between 2,000 and 6,000 feet on the western slope.

INFORMATION
For years, California nutmeg was known as Torreya, named for John Torrey, a noted botanist who held professorships concurrently at both Columbia and Princeton Universities. It is called nutmeg because of the similarity of its aromatic seeds to those of the unrelated tropical species (*Myristica*), from which commercial nutmeg is obtained. The other common name, "Stinking-cedar," alludes to the disagreeable odor of its resinous foliage (and other parts) when crushed.

Because of its resemblance to Douglas-fir and white fir, California nutmeg is one of the most misidentified trees in the Sierra. It generally occupies areas too hot and exposed for those other species, its conspicuous blue-green rounded fruits differ greatly from woody fir cones, and its sharp-pointed needles are unlike those of Douglas-fir or white fir.

Some of the best places to observe this species are along Highway 140 between El Portal and Yosemite Valley, and at the entrance to Boyden Cave in Kings Canyon.

SIMILAR SPECIES
Douglas-fir and white fir (see above).

ASSOCIATED SPECIES
Because of its patchy distribution, it is not typically associated with other species.

DESCRIPTION

- **Size:** medium-sized tree, 20 to 70 feet (6-21 m)
- **Bark:** thin, green on young branches, gray-brown on older ones
- **Needles:** 1 to 2.75 inches (2.5-5.7 cm), shiny dark green above with two narrow whitish lines beneath, slightly curved, sharply pointed at tip, aromatic
- **Fruit:** 1 to 1.5 inches (2.5-4 cm), plum-like, with greenish or purplish covering; male cones are on separate trees
- **Shape:** irregular (not symmetrical like firs) with many downward sweeping sprays

Pacific Yew

Taxus brevifolia

HABITAT & RANGE

Uncommon in moist, well-shaded areas north of Yosemite on the western slope between 2,500 and 4,000 feet. Individual trees have been observed in the southern Sierra around Sequoia National Park between 5,000 and 8,000 feet.

INFORMATION

The most distinguishing feature of the yew is its bright red fruit. No other evergreen has a crimson fruit with a single, dark seed on the inside. The berries are a preferred food for many types of birds. The seed, however, is toxic. Most birds simply pass the seeds through their digestive tracts, aiding the tree's dispersal in so doing. The foliage is toxic as well. The bark, on the other hand, contains taxol, a promising cancer-killing agent.

This species prefers shade. Because of its small size and green twigs, it is difficult to confuse with other evergreens, especially if the fruit is out. Extremely slow-growing, yews with a trunk of twelve inches in diameter are estimated to be about 150 years old.

SIMILAR SPECIES

California nutmeg. Nutmeg's needles are stiff with sharp pointed tips. Those of the yew are soft and flexible. Additionally, nutmeg has white lines on the undersurface of its needles, yews do not.

ASSOCIATED SPECIES

Due to its low abundance, the yew is not typically associated with a general forest type.

DESCRIPTION

- **Size:** shrubby to small tree up to 25 feet (7 m)
- **Bark:** reddish to brownish, thin, smooth and peeling with age
- **Needles:** evergreen, single, 0.5 to 1 inch (1-2.4 cm), soft and flexible, similar green color on both sides
- **Cones:** on separate trees - male cones are tiny, 0.125 inch, and pale yellow; female cones are bright red berries, about 0.5 inch long
- **Fruit:** red berry
- **Other:** green twigs

White Fir

Abies concolor

HABITAT & RANGE

Common on moist, rocky mountain soils in the Ponderosa Pine Belt across the Sierra from 3,000 to 8,000 feet, occasionally as high as 10,000 feet.

INFORMATION

White and California red firs are the only "true" members of the fir family in the Sierra, a group typically associated with cold climates. Their cylindrical shape is an adaptation for shedding heavy snow. Distinguishing characteristics are bark with resin blisters (filled with oily balsam) and cones that sit upright. The cones disintegrate with time (intact cones on the ground quickly deteriorate) unlike those of other conifers.

The white fir does not produce cones annually; heavy crops appear between three and nine years. Growth is slow for the first 30 years; afterwards, it becomes rapid. A young tree's age can be determined by the number of whorls around its base. Some trees are known to have lived for five hundred years.

Although too bitter for human consumption, fir seeds are utilized by many songbird and mammal species. Buds of the tree are eaten by grouse, young twigs and needles by deer. The heartwood is susceptible to fungal infestations, which are responsible for the death of many old trees. Bears, however, will hibernate in the hollowed fir logs.

SIMILAR SPECIES

California red fir (see pg. 48) and Douglas-fir. Note the latter's distinct cone and sharp, pointed terminal bud.

ASSOCIATED SPECIES

Several, see pg. 114 under "Ponderosa Pine/Mixed Coniferous Belt."

DESCRIPTION

- **Size:** large tree, 70 to 180 feet (20-60 m)
- **Bark:** on young trees is grayish-white and smooth becoming much darker and furrowed with age
- **Needles:** grow singly, light blue-green with white lines on both sides, 1 to 2.5 inches (2.5-6 cm), quarter twist at base, flat, flexible, two-sided, some spread to the sides, others curve upward
- **Cones:** 3 to 5 inches (7.5-13 cm), cylindrical, purple or yellow
- **Shape:** tapering, narrow, pointed crown, branches evenly spaced on the trunk, overall symmetrical appearance

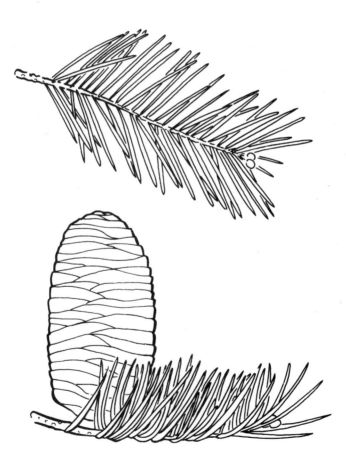

California Red Fir

Red Fir, Silver Fir
Abies magnifica

HABITAT & RANGE

Common on moist, western slopes, often in pure stands between 6,000 and 9,500 feet. It is found on the east slope south of the Mammoth Lakes area.

INFORMATION

California red fir gets its name from its deep red inner bark, easily observed by flaking off some outer bark. Young firs are shade tolerant and grow very slowly the first few years of life; ten-year-old seedlings may be just one foot tall. Saplings are often deformed by the weight of snow. They also have low germination rates. One study reported that only 4% of the seeds that reached the ground grew successfully.

Also, mature trees can be infested with a pathogenic fungus, a parasitic dwarf mistletoe, and a specialized fir engraver beetle (*Scolytus*). Despite these pests and slow growth and germination rates, California red fir apparently maintains its presence by being long-lived (up to 350 years).

A variety, Shasta red fir, is virtually indistinguishable from California red fir, except for its long, pointed bracts that occur between the scales of its cones. Common in Sequoia and Kings Canyon National Parks, it is absent in the Yosemite area. Both types (which apparently hybridize) are observed north of Yosemite to Mt. Shasta.

SIMILAR SPECIES

White fir (see pg. 46), and Douglas-fir. California red fir is found above 6,000 feet and Douglas-fir does not grow

DESCRIPTION
- **Size:** large tree 60 to 160 feet (20-60 m)
- **Bark:** young bark is smooth and white, becoming furrowed with age; inner bark is deep red, outer scales are dark red or purplish
- **Needles:** blue-green, roundish, 0.75 to 1.75 inches (2-3.5 cm), single, four-sided, crowded and curved upward at the tip
- **Cones:** 6 to 8 inches (15-20 cm) purplish-brown, scales with fine hairs; a variety (A. *magnifica var. shastensis*) has long, pointed bracts between the scales
- **Shape:** mature trees have a flat crown with narrow tapering branches, young trees grow more symmetrically

above 5,500 feet. The cones and buds of Douglas-fir are distinctive (see pg. 50).

ASSOCIATED SPECIES
California red fir most often occur in pure stands, but Jeffrey, lodgepole, and western white pines, and an occasional western juniper, can be seen on the edges of the fir forest.

Douglas-fir

Pseudotsuga menziesii

HABITAT & RANGE
Moderately common, it prefers moist well-drained soils of the western slope between 3,500 and 5,500 feet, but will grow slightly below and above this where suitable conditions exist. It does not grow much south of Yosemite National Park and is absent in Kings Canyon and Sequoia National Parks.

INFORMATION
Besides the cones and branch tips, bark can be used to distinguish the Douglas-fir from the red and white firs. California red fir has deep red inner bark, white fir bark is yellowish-brown, and Douglas-fir has inner bark in layers of white and red.

Douglas-fir has the distinction of being the number one lumber producing tree in the nation. Although most of the production today comes out of Washington and Oregon, a number of California's giants were toppled at the turn of the century. A few large individuals are still protected in Yosemite.

Because it is out-competed by other trees, Douglas-fir depends on periodic fires and insect attacks to open up the forest and allow new growth.

A fast-growing tree that prefers north facing slopes and canyons in the Sierra, Douglas-fir is known for its high annual seed production, with exceptional crops every three to four years. Individuals can live for up to 700 years, with the record being 1,385 years.

SIMILAR SPECIES
White and California red fir. Firs have upright cones and small, rounded terminal buds, while Douglas-fir has drooping cones and a long, pointed terminal bud.

DESCRIPTION

- **Size:** large tree, 80 to 200 feet (24-60 m)
- **Bark:** smooth and grayish with resin blisters when young, but becoming deeply furrowed and darker with age, inner bark in layers of white and red
- **Needles:** about 1 inch (2.5 cm), flattened, growing on all sides of branchlets
- **Cones:** 2 to 3.5 inches (5-9 cm), light brown, with conspicuous three-pointed bracts between the cone scales
- **Shape:** narrow, pointed crown and slightly drooping

ASSOCIATED SPECIES

See pg. 114 under "Ponderosa Pine/Mixed Coniferous Belt."

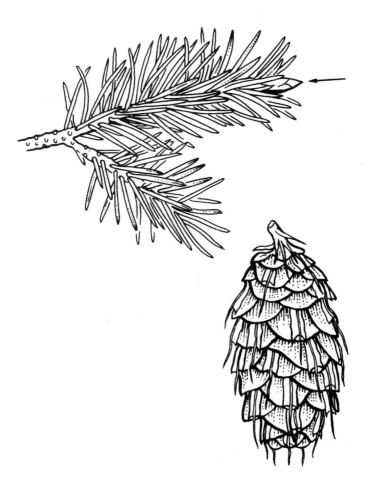

Mountain Hemlock

Tsuga mertensiana

HABITAT & RANGE

Common on both sides of the Sierra in moist soils (often on north-facing slopes) between 6,000 and 11,000 feet, north of Kings Canyon National Park.

INFORMATION

Unlike those of the firs, mountain hemlock needles occur on all sides of its branches. The woody projection at the base of each needle is also distinctive (see right).

Mountain hemlock generally is found in areas with the heaviest snowfall. The long, drooping top and soft, light wood are believed to be adaptations to shed snow and to avoid breaking from its weight.

Individuals have lived for 400 to 500 years. Hemlock grows slowly (trees with a twenty inch diameter may be 250 years old), but is a prolific seed producer. During exceptional years, cones can be so numerous they weigh down the branches. The seeds have large wings and are easily dispersed by the wind. Reproduction may also occur if lower branches become rooted due to heavy snow. These branches eventually grow into separate trees.

Hemlock groves provide cover for many species of birds and mammals.

SIMILAR SPECIES

The only single-needled conifer also growing within the range of the hemlock is California red fir. Note drooping top of mountain hemlock.

ASSOCIATED SPECIES

Whitebark and lodgepole pines, California red fir.

DESCRIPTION

■ **Size:** medium-sized tree, 30 to 100 feet (9-30 m)
■ **Bark:** gray to dark brown, developing deep fissures with age
■ **Needles:** blue-green, stiff, 0.5 to 1 inch (0.7-2.5 cm), attached at base to tiny, woody projections, usually growing upward on all sides of the branches
■ **Cones:** cylindrical, 1 to 3 inches (2.5-7.5 cm), soft, immature cones are purplish turning brown with age, hang down
■ **Shape:** slender conical crown with pronounced drooping top

Singleleaf Pinyon Pine

Singleleaf Pine, Pinyon
Pinus monophylla

HABITAT & RANGE:
  Common on dry, rocky slopes and ridges of eastern Sierra
(mostly below 9,000 feet) from Mono Lake region south.
Found in a few scattered places on the western slope
including granite ridges between Tiltill Valley and
Rancheria Creek in Yosemite National Park, and on the
south-facing wall above Cedar Grove in Kings Canyon
National Park.

INFORMATION
  Singleleaf, unlike any of our other native pines, has only
one needle. Like its relatives, however, this pine grows a
papery sheath at the base of the needles on its new twigs.
A microscopic look at a cross section of a singleleaf needle
reveals five separate vascular bundles. This suggests that at
one time the species had five needles that later fused as
one.
  The small, nutritious seeds of the singleleaf were and
continue to be an important food source for Paiute and
other Indian people of the Great Basin in Nevada and eastern California. The Navajo of the American Southwest
harvest edible seeds from the Colorado pinyon (*Pinus
edulis*). The nuts of both species are gathered and sold
today without distinction.
  The seeds are also integral to the diets of many kinds of
wildlife such as jays, chipmunks, and woodrats. Pinyon jays
have been known to collect as many as 40 nuts in their
throats before flying off to bury their loads at distances up
to five miles away!

SIMILAR SPECIES
  None. California nutmeg also bears a single leaf that
slightly resembles that of the singleleaf pine. The nutmeg's

DESCRIPTION

- **Size:** small tree, 16 to 30 feet (5-9 m), often shrubby
- **Shape:** generally low with rounded crown, trunks often bent or forked; trees are typically well-spaced, resembling old orchards
- **Bark:** dark brown to gray becoming furrowed with age
- **Needles:** single, 1 to 2.25 inches (3-5 cm), dull gray-green, stout, sharp-pointed
- **Cones:** 2 to 3 inches (3-6 cm) long, oval, resinous, with thick scales
- **Other:** often individual trees well-spaced out

needles are strongly aromatic when crushed, and its range does not overlap the singleleaf's.

ASSOCIATED SPECIES

Jeffrey pine, western juniper, and curl-leaf mountain-mahogany.

Incense Cedar

Calocedrus decurrens

HABITAT & RANGE
Common throughout the west slope of the Sierra mostly below 7,000 feet.

INFORMATION
This tree has undergone several name changes since it was first discovered. Today botanists place it in its own group, *Calocedrus*, literally meaning "cedars from California." There are no true "cedars" in America (true cedars were first described in Syria and Asia Minor), and so the name is sometimes hyphenated or enclosed in quotations.

The most distinguishing feature of the incense cedar is its aromatic wood and leaves. The wood, although noted for its durability, is susceptible as it ages to dry rot fungus (*Polyporus amarus*) that enters through old fire scars. The primary commercial use for incense cedar today is in the manufacture of pencils.

The pollen of the tree is shed in winter, causing allergies in some people. High seed production under favorable conditions occurs every two to three years.

SIMILAR SPECIES
Giant sequoia. Incense cedar leaves are flattened, and aromatic, those of the sequoia are not.

ASSOCIATED SPECIES
Several, see pg. 114 under "Ponderosa Pine/Mixed Coniferous Belt."

DESCRIPTION

- **Size:** large tree, 60 to 150 feet (18-46 m)
- **Bark:** cinnamon brown and deeply furrowed
- **Needles:** small, only 0.25 to 0.5 inch (0.3-1.2 cm), overlapping each other and extending down the twig, aromatic when crushed and shiny green
- **Cones:** nearly an inch long with two woody scales that split lengthwise when ripe to expose winged seeds
- **Shape:** young trees are triangular and symmetrical, older trees develop an irregular, often flat top

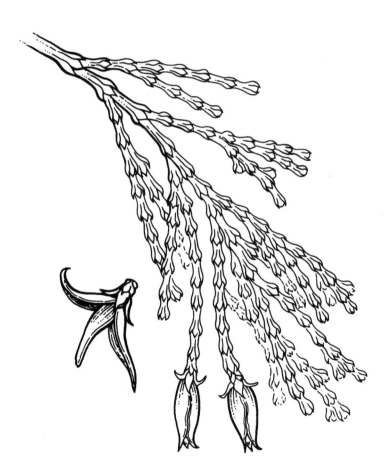

Giant Sequoia

Sequoiadendron giganteum

HABITAT & RANGE

Rare, but locally common in seventy-five scattered groves along the western slope between 5,000 and 7,000 feet.

INFORMATION

The coast redwood (*Sequoia sempervirens*) is the world's tallest tree, attaining heights of 390 feet, and an individual bald cypress (*Taxodium distichum*) in Florida has the largest base of any tree in North America. But in terms of total volume of wood the giant sequoia is unrivalled. A single sequoia may contain more wood than is found on an acre of a fine virgin forest in the Pacific Northwest.

The sequoia is not only the world's largest tree, but also one of the fastest growing and oldest. Each year it adds the equivalent of the volume of a tree 60 feet tall and 1.5 feet in diameter to its bulk! The oldest big trees are around 3,000 years old.

Despite its colossal size and amazing longevity, the giant sequoia is a relatively rare tree, found only on the western slope of the Sierra Nevada. Fossil evidence shows that these monarchs were once common throughout much of the world dating from sixty million years ago.

SIMILAR SPECIES

Incense cedar. The flattened scalelike needles of the incense cedar, not prickly to the touch, are distinctly different from the sharp, pointed needles of the sequoia.

ASSOCIATED SPECIES

Incense cedar, Pacific ponderosa and sugar pines, white fir, and mountain dogwood.

DESCRIPTION

■ **Size:** the world's largest tree, 150 to 250 feet (46-76 m), 10 to 25 feet in diameter at the base

■ **Bark:** thick, fibrous, spongy, cinnamon-red, often with burn scars

■ **Needles:** scale-like, overlapping, 0.1 to 0.2 inch (0.3-0.6 cm), sharp-pointed, blue-green

■ **Cones:** 1.5 to 3 inches (4.5-7.5 cm), elliptical, reddish-brown; immature cones are closed, yellow to dark green

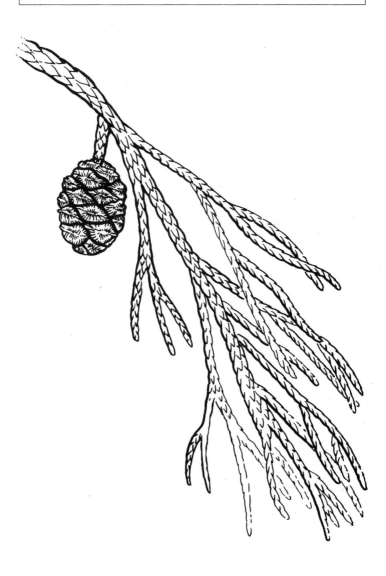

Western Juniper

Sierra Juniper
Juniperus occidentalis
var. occidentalis

HABITAT & RANGE
Locally common in dry habitats along the western and eastern slope from 7,000 to 10,500 feet.

INFORMATION
While the giant sequoia is well-known for its longevity, few people realize that western junipers attain ages as old as the big trees. Some junipers in the Yosemite area are believed to be at least two thousand years old. One tree near Sonora Pass is estimated to have been growing over three thousand years.

The bark of juniper is distinctive in the way it spirals around the tree. Spiralling is a phenomenon found in other species of trees inhabiting harsh, windy areas (i.e. the foxtail pine). It has been suggested that a spiral grain adds strength and resistance to strong winds.

This species is easily recognized by its cones. They are not woody like those of most Sierran evergreens, but fleshy and resembling berries. Animals play an important role in the dispersal of junipers as the large seeds are not easily windblown.

SIMILAR SPECIES
California and common juniper. California juniper (*J. californica*) is a large shrub (1-4 m) found on dry, rocky slopes below 5,000 feet on the western slope. It can be distinguished from western juniper by its red rather than bluish-black berries, and its more deeply infolded trunk. Common juniper (*J. communis*) is a common shrub above 6,500 feet from Mono Pass north. It rarely attains heights over one meter.

DESCRIPTION

- **Size:** small to medium-sized evergreen tree with short trunk, 15 to 70 feet (5-21 m)
- **Bark:** reddish-brown, shreddy, furrowed, frequently spiraled
- **Needles:** scale-like, tiny (.06 inch) and overlapping each other, and the gray-green foliage is usually covered with white resin on its underside
- **Cone:** berry-like, blue-black, soft, juicy, resinous
- **Shape:** solitary, often with dead or missing branches

ASSOCIATED SPECIES
Several, see pg. 115 under "Red Fir/Lodgepole Pine Belt."

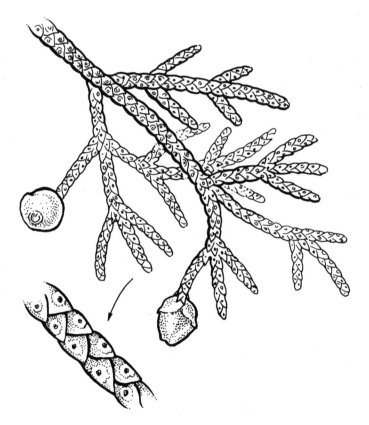

Sierra Bladdernut

Staphylea bolanderi

HABITAT & RANGE
Uncommon, on canyon walls of the west slope mostly north of Sequoia National Forest between 1,000 and 4,500 feet.

INFORMATION
This species is easily overlooked and never abundant. Finding it can be challenging. A good place to look is near the Arch Rock Entrance Station to Yosemite National Park along Highway 140. It prefers full sunlight and will grow on a variety of soil types.

No other tree in the Sierra has a bladder-shaped fruit, which distinguishes this species.

SIMILAR SPECIES
Foothill and Oregon ash. Both of these species, however, have five to seven leaflets.

ASSOCIATED SPECIES
Too uncommon to be associated with particular species.

DESCRIPTION

■ **Size:** shrubbish, rarely a small tree up to 15 feet
■ **Bark:** gray to brown
■ **Leaves:** compound, made up of 3 oval to nearly circular leaflets, each 1 to 2 inches long, margins finely serrated
■ **Fruit:** papery, inflated (like a bladder), 1 to 2 inches long

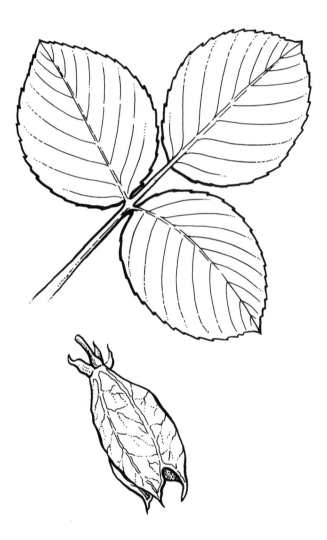

California Buckeye

Aesculus californica

HABITAT & RANGE
Common on the western slope along stream borders on hillsides throughout the Sierra up to 3,500 feet.

INFORMATION
California buckeye is shrub-like; often several stems will arise from a common root. Its flowers bloom in May and June.

The raw seeds of the buckeye are poisonous, but California Indians leached the seeds, then ground them into flour for cooking. Unleached seeds had another native use. Fish were diverted into pools with the use of rock walls, and ground buckeye seeds were thrown into the water. The seeds released chemicals that stupefied the fish, which could then be collected with minimal effort.

By midsummer the tree has shed its leaves and entered dormancy in preparation for the hot, dry months ahead. With the leaves absent, the pear-shaped fruits, containing one large, two-inch seed, hang noticeably.

The resemblance of the glossy brown seed to the eye of a male deer is the probable origin for the popular name "buckeye."

SIMILAR SPECIES
None.

ASSOCIATED SPECIES
Interior live oak, gray pine.

DESCRIPTION

- **Size:** large bush or tree, to 25 feet (7.5 m)
- **Bark:** light-gray, thin, and smooth
- **Leaves:** composed of 7 leaflets (sometimes 5), 3 to 7 inches long, spreading like fingers from a hand (palmate), on a long, 4 to 5 inch leaf stem
- **Fruit:** 2 to 3 inches (5-7.5 m), pale brown, smooth, leathery, and pear-shaped, maturing in late summer

Oregon Ash

Fraxinus latifolia

HABITAT & RANGE

Locally common at streamsides in canyons on the western slope below 5,000 feet throughout the Sierra.

INFORMATION

Ashes, like lilacs and forsythias, are members of the olive family. All have their leaves arranged opposite each other, usually with male and female flowers on separate plants. In April or May, the leaves and flower buds unfold; occasionally, the flowers actually open before the leaves. The leaves, made up of leaflets, are arranged in pairs with a single terminal leaflet; accordingly, the total number of leaflets per leaf is always odd (see diagram).

The most distinguishing feature of ashes is their winged-fruits, called "samaras," which look like the blades of miniature canoe paddles. Their wings allow them to be carried a considerable distance from their parent tree. Mice and other small rodents eat the seeds. In the Pacific Northwest, Oregon ash grows considerably larger and is logged commercially.

SIMILAR SPECIES

California or two-petal ash. Oregon ash is taller, has rounded stems (opposed to the 4-angled twigs of California ash), and larger leaves. The leaf margins of California ash are more sharply serrated.

ASSOCIATED SPECIES

Pacific ponderosa pine, willow, cottonwood.

NOTE

California ash (*Fraxinus diptela*) grows from 5 to 15 feet (2.5 m) on the dry west slope of the southern Sierra between 1,500 and 3,500 feet, primarily in foothills, chaparral, and woodlands. Notice the four-angled twigs instead of the usual round ones found on most trees. Its flower,

DESCRIPTION

■ **Size:** short tree, up to 30 feet (12.5 m), with a long, straight trunk

■ **Bark:** dark gray or brown, developing cracks and thickening with age

■ **Leaves:** 5 to 12 inches (13-30 cm) and made up of several (5 to 7) smaller leaves, 2 to 5 inches (5-13 cm), attached in rows to the central stalk (pinnately compound). The leaf margins of the smaller leaves are wavy or smooth.

■ **Fruit:** light brown, 1.25 to 2 inches (3-5 cm), usually hanging in dense clusters (resembling miniature canoe paddles)

although not fragrant, is distinctive (see diagram), consisting of two white, drooping petals. It is eaten by mule deer. California ash is uncommon throughout the Sierra, but locally common in Sequoia-Kings Canyon National Parks.

California ash

Western Sycamore

California Sycamore, Buttonball, Buttonwood
Platanus racemosa

HABITAT & RANGE

Locally common in wet soils along streams and canyons in foothills extending up to about 3,000 feet on the western slope of the central and southern Sierra.

INFORMATION

Sycamore's bark is highly distinctive among trees throughout the world. Instead of becoming thick with age, it peels annually, keeping a smooth and conspicuously white appearance. Scientists suspect this trait carries over from nearly 100 million years ago. Sycamore trees have been found as far north as the Arctic Circle.

The white wooly hairs on the underside of the leaves, shed annually, cause allergies in some people. Due to its interesting flowers and fruits, which look like a string of balls, sycamore has also been called "buttonball" or "buttonwood."

SIMILAR SPECIES

Maple. The smooth, peeling white bark of the sycamore sets it apart.

ASSOCIATED SPECIES

Valley oak.

DESCRIPTION

- **Size:** medium-sized tree, 40 to 80 feet (12-24 m)
- **Bark:** white and smooth, peeling into brownish flakes, becoming furrowed at base with age
- **Leaves:** similar shape to maple, 6 to 9 inches (15-23 cm) long and wide
- **Fruit:** consists of 2 to 7 balls, or heads, (0.75 inch wide) that hang on a long stalk

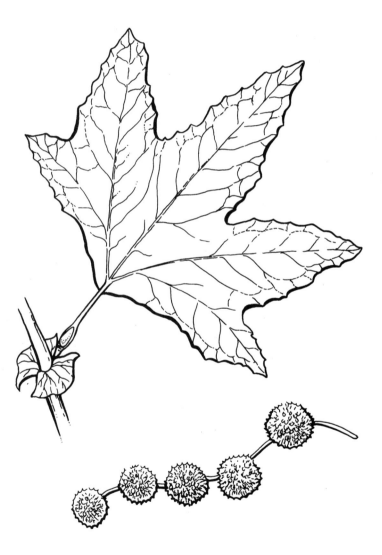

Blue Oak

Iron Oak, Mountain White Oak
Quercus douglasii

HABITAT & RANGE
   Common on western slopes up to 3,000 feet throughout the Sierra in dry or gravelly places.

INFORMATION
   Blue oak is one of the most widely distributed hardwood trees in California, covering over two million acres. It thrives on the driest slopes of the Sierra and is typically the last foothill tree to unfurl its leaves.
   At present, there is a lack of regeneration of this species in the foothills. It appears that fire is essential for the success of new trees, and there has been a recent history of fire suppression in blue oak habitat. Unsuccessful regeneration may be due also to an increase in browsing by livestock and deer, or simply to the shading out of younger trees by older ones.
   Blue oak wood is close-grained and heavy. Many an axe has been dulled on this species that early settlers dubbed "iron oak."

SIMILAR SPECIES
   None.

ASSOCIATED SPECIES
   Gray pine, interior live oak.

DESCRIPTION

- **Size:** small to medium-sized tree, 20 to 60 feet (6-18 m)
- **Bark:** light gray and scaly
- **Leaves:** pale green above, even paler beneath, 1.25 to 4 inches (3-10 cm) long, 0.75 to 1.75 inches (2-4.5 cm) wide, with 4 to 5 shallow, rounded lobes. The leaf margins are mostly smooth, but may have fine, serrated edges
- **Fruit:** slender acorn, 0.75 to 1.75 inches (2-4.5 cm)
- **Other:** hairy twigs

Valley Oak

California White Oak, Valley White Oak, Roble
Quercus lobata

HABITAT & RANGE

Formerly common in valleys and on slopes with rich loam soils, forming groves in foothills, up to 4,000 feet in the southern Sierra.

INFORMATION

Valley oak is the largest and tallest of all North American oaks. Unique to California's Central Valley and Sierra foothills, it prefers rich, deep soil associated with stream and river floodplains. Early settlers discovered that valley oaks were indicators of prime soils, ideal for farmland. Today, major cities in the Central Valley (Visalia, Stockton, Sacramento, Chico) are established where large valley oak groves once existed. Only a small percentage of the trees that formerly covered the valley remains, and most of the present groves lack saplings and seedlings.

An unanticipated factor contributing to the demise of the oaks has been the construction of dams on major rivers draining into the central valley. These prevent massive winter and spring floods, formerly responsible for delivering nutrient-rich silt to the valley oak forest. The current decline of the valley oak is due mainly to changes in land use management.

SIMILAR SPECIES

None.

ASSOCIATED SPECIES

Mostly grassland species.

DESCRIPTION

- **Size:** large tree from 40 to 100 feet (12-30 m)
- **Bark:** light gray or brown, thick, and deeply furrowed
- **Leaves:** dark green above, paler beneath, small, only 2 to 4 inches (5-10 cm), and 1 to 3 inches wide, with 7 to 11 deep lobes which extend more than halfway to the leaf center
- **Fruit:** acorn, 1.25 to 2.25 inches (3-6 cm)
- **Other:** twigs are hairless

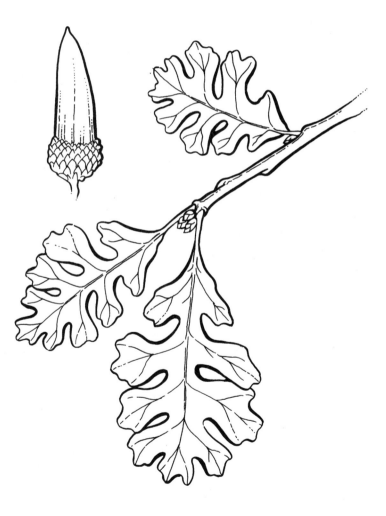

California Black Oak

Black Oak, Kelloggs Oak
Quercus kelloggii

HABITAT & RANGE
Common on the west slope to 7,000 feet throughout the Sierra.

INFORMATION
California Indians depended on the black oak for survival. Tribes gathered and stored hundreds of pounds of acorns in *chukahs* (granaries). The acorns were ground and leached (to eliminate the bitter tannic acid) before being cooked in a large basket using rocks heated in a fire. The resulting mush is high in fat and nutrition.

Black oak acorns (which occur in enormous crops every few years) are also eaten by deer, gray squirrels, band-tailed pigeons, acorn woodpeckers, and other wildlife. Survival of the black oak is tenuous as it is extremely intolerant of shade. Without natural or prescribed fire or other forest-clearing disturbances, black oak will become dominated by conifers.

This has occurred in Yosemite Valley where fire has been suppressed for many decades. Park managers are developing ways to protect existing oaks and to promote the establishment of new seedlings.

SIMILAR SPECIES
None. The only oak with bristle-tipped margins.

ASSOCIATED SPECIES
Pacific ponderosa pine, incense cedar, white fir, canyon live oak, big-leaf maple, and mountain dogwood.

DESCRIPTION

- **Size:** medium-sized tree 30 to 80 feet (10-25 m)
- **Bark:** thick, dark brown, becoming furrowed into irregular plates
- **Leaves:** 3 to 8 inches (7.5-20 cm), about half as wide, with 5-7 lobes, each with a few bristle-pointed teeth
- **Fruit:** acorn, 1 to 1.5 inches (2.5-4 cm), elliptical, with a thin, scaly cup

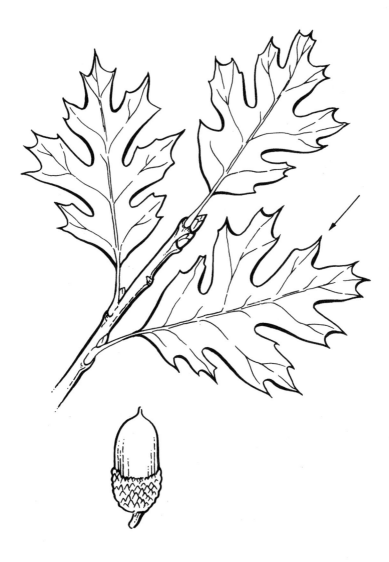

Big-leaf Maple

Broadleaf Maple
Acer macrophyllum

HABITAT & RANGE

Common along stream banks in moist canyons of the west slope throughout the Sierra up to 5,500 feet.

INFORMATION

Big-leaf maple has the largest leaves (6 to 12 inches) of any North American maple, and produces extraordinary numbers of seeds year after year. The winged seeds (samaras) can be seen hanging from the trees throughout the winter. They are eaten by mice, woodrats, squirrels, chipmunks, and birds.

Seedlings are common beneath the forest canopy, but as few as one in a million will meet with favorable conditions and grow into a large tree. Once established, big-leaf maples live for two hundred years.

Large numbers of insects are attracted to the small, yellow, sweet-scented flowers that usually develop before the leaves open in early May. The leaves of big-leaf maple are susceptible to a speckled tar spot fungus (*Rhytisima punctatus*) that causes numerous tar-brown colored spots. These markings become prevalent during late summer and early fall when the leaves turn yellow or orange.

The stump of a newly-cut or broken big-leaf maple will send up many shoots from its base, a sprouting ability common in many tree species. These shoots are a preferred food of mule deer.

SIMILAR SPECIES

None.

ASSOCIATED SPECIES

Cottonwood, mountain dogwood, incense cedar, Pacific ponderosa pine, canyon live oak.

DESCRIPTION

- **Size:** small to medium-sized tree, 30 to 70 feet (9-21 m)
- **Bark:** dark gray to brown, becoming furrowed and separated with age
- **Leaves:** very large, 6 to 12 inches (15-30 cm) long and wide, with 5 (sometimes only 3) deep lobes. The leafstalk is very long, 8 to 12 inches (20-30 cm), and contains a milky, white sap
- **Fruit:** single fruits called samaras (1.5 to 2 inches long) are paired, forming a "V" shape

NOTE

Mountain maple (*Acer glabrum*) grows more as a multi-stemmed shrub (10 to 15 feet) than a tree. It is found on both slopes of the central and southern Sierra, preferring moist slopes usually between 5,000 and 9,000 feet. It can be distinguished from big-leaf maple by its smaller leaves (1 to 2 inches wide) and bright reddish buds and twigs.

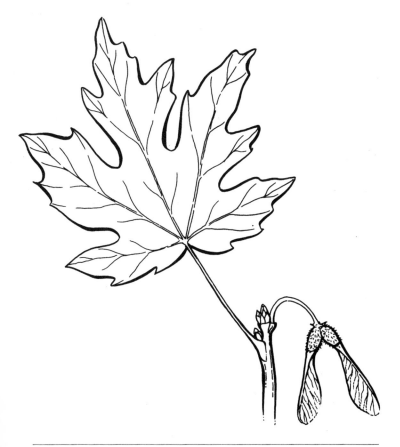

Birch-leaf Mountain-Mahogany

Birchleaf Cercocarpus, Hardtack
Cercocarpus betuloides var. betuloides

HABITAT & RANGE
Common on dry, rocky slopes and in foothill washes on the western slope throughout the Sierra below 6,000 feet.

INFORMATION
Better classed as a shrub than as a tree, this species is included because it is common on the west slope of the Sierra and occasionally grows large under favorable conditions. It is primarily a chaparral shrub, sprouting back after fire, but it is seen occasionally beneath a stand of mixed conifers. The genus, "*Cercocarpus*," comes from the Greek words for "tail" and "fruit" and refers to the hairy tails or plumes attached to the seed. The leaves superficially resemble those of shrub-like birches from which the name is derived. Once called "hardtack," birch-leaf mountain-mahogany can withstand cutting, fire, drought, and heavy browsing by deer.

SIMILAR SPECIES
None.

ASSOCIATED SPECIES
See "Ponderosa Pine/Mixed Coniferous Belt" on page 114.

DESCRIPTION

- **Size:** large shrub to small tree, 10 to 20 feet (3-6 m)
- **Bark:** mostly smooth, dark brown, turning scaly with age
- **Leaves:** 1 to 1.25 inches (2.5-3 cm), about half as wide, with distinctly serrated margins, and parallel veins
- **Fruit:** tiny and one-seeded, with prominent 1.5- to 4-inch-long white, hairy tails attached

Interior Live Oak

Sierra Live Oak
Quercus wislizenii

HABITAT & RANGE
   Common on dry slopes and valleys throughout the
Sierra, mostly between 1,500 and 4,000 feet.

INFORMATION
   As a group, oaks are known for their ability to form
hybrids, and the interior live oak is no exception. In areas
where they overlap, interior live oak will produce a hybrid
with black oak, commonly called "oracle oak." Its leaves
are two to five inches long with shallow lobes.
   One might expect that the strong, heavy wood would
have been used by settlers or commercially logged, but this
did not occur. The tree's long, large limbs grow out and
down around the trunk making access difficult and creating
knotty wood. As a result, these large, beautiful "nature
domes" will probably provide much-needed shade to the
weary traveller of the future.
   When closely examined, leaves of live oak species will
often have unusual looking growths, called "galls." Over
fifty kinds of insects cause galls to form on the leaves.
Their bizarre shapes and colors are astonishing.

SIMILAR SPECIES
   Canyon live oak.

ASSOCIATED SPECIES
   Blue oak, gray pine.

DESCRIPTION

- **Size:** medium-sized tree, 30 to 70 feet (9-21 m)
- **Bark:** dark gray to brown, becoming scaly with age
- **Leaves:** evergreen, dark green and shiny above, lighter green below, 1 to 2 inches (2.5-5 cm) long, 0.5 to 1.25 inches (1.2-3 cm) wide; two types of leaves may be present on the same tree; some leaf margins will have smooth edges, others sharp spiny edges
- **Fruit:** slender acorn, 0.75 to 2 inches (2-4 m)
- **Other:** tree is often twice as broad as tall due to the long limbs that extend out from the trunk and create a dome effect

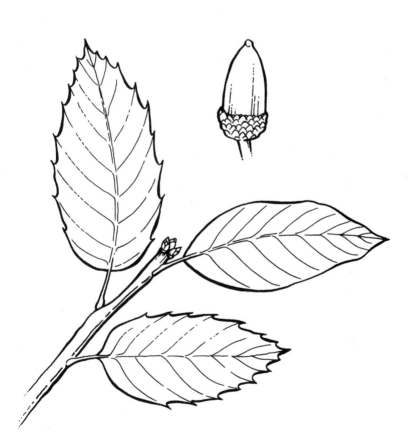

Canyon Live Oak

Goldencup Oak, Maul Oak
Quercus chrysolepis

HABITAT & RANGE
   Common in canyons and moist slopes throughout the
Sierra mostly between 3,500 and 6,500 feet.

INFORMATION
   Two species of live oaks (canyon and interior) grow in
the Sierra. They are so named because they do not drop
their leaves annually like deciduous oaks, remaining green
year-round. Although the two species are similar, they can
be differentiated by acorn size and shape, presence or
absence of hair on the undersurface of the leaf, elevation,
and habitat. Canyon live oak prefers deep canyons with
steep walls while interior live oak prefers the hot, grassy
slopes and rolling foothills. Interior live oaks can be
observed growing near stands of gray pine or blue oak.
   Canyon oaks grow taller when clinging precipitously to
steep walls than when growing in the open landscape.
They can form large dome-shaped crowns that may extend
125 feet. The wood of the tree is extremely tough and
strong, three times sturdier than that of the mighty sequoia.
The wood was a favorite of pioneers for the heads of mauls,
hence the common name "maul oak." Settlers also used
the wood for axles, wagon wheels, tool handles, and ship's
frames.

SIMILAR SPECIES
   Interior live oak.

ASSOCIATED SPECIES
   See "Ponderosa Pine/Mixed Coniferous Belt" on page
114.

DESCRIPTION

■ **Size:** medium-sized tree, 20 to 80 feet (6-24 m)
■ **Bark:** light gray, slightly furrowed (sometimes smooth)
■ **Leaves:** thick and leathery, evergreen, holly-like, 1 to 3 inches (2.4-7.5 cm) long and about half as wide, often with two different types of leaves on the same tree
■ **Fruit:** acorn, 0.75 to 2 inches (2-5 cm) long, variable in shape, with yellowish hairs or fuzz on the cup

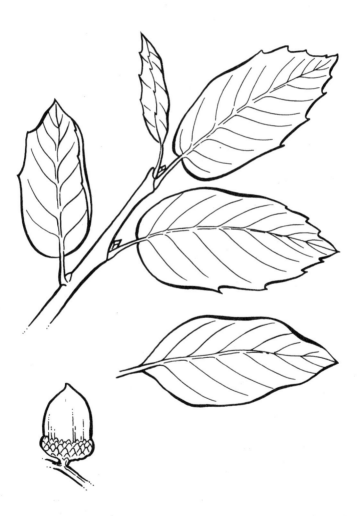

Willow

Salix sp.

The large genus of willows (*Salix*), typically associated with wet soils, includes shrubs and mostly small trees. Of the two dozen or so willows found in the Sierra, about five are more tree-like in their habits and are mentioned briefly below (for more information see Philip Munz's *California Flora* or *The Jepson Manual*, edited by James Hickman).

While it is easy to distinguish willows from other trees and shrubs by their long, narrow, simple (not compound or divided) leaves, brightly colored yellow to reddish twigs, and narrow clusters of catkins or "pussy willows," which bloom before the leaves appear in the spring, it can be a challenge to the trained botanist to identify the different types. Willow seeds are fast germinating – they grow within twenty-four hours of being shed! Willows also reproduce through sprouting from old roots and stumps. Twigs of various willow are used by California Indians for making baskets.

Scouler's willow (*S. scouleriana*) differs from other willows in that it can establish itself away from water. It grows to 10,000 feet in the Sierra. Its leaves (2 to 5 inches) are broadest at the middle (0.5 to 1.5 inches) and have smooth leaf margins; they are dark green above with white, gray, or red hairs beneath. The red hairs distinguish the Scouler's from other willows. Twigs are very hairy when young, and stripped bark has a skunk-like odor. Reaching 30 feet in height on occasion, it is sometimes called "fire willow" because it rapidly occupies burned areas. It is named for its Scottish discoverer, John Scouler.

Arroyo willow (*S. lasiolepsis*) can be distinguished from other willows by the white blotches it has on its young bark and limbs. Found strictly along watercourses as high as 7,000 feet, it is common along the Middle Fork of the

Kaweah River and at Mineral King in Sequoia National Park. Its leaves (2 to 5 inches long, 0.5 to 1 inch wide) are often thick and leathery, dark green and hairless above, whitish below, and usually hairy beneath.

Shining willow (*S. lucida ssp. lasiandra*) is best identified by its long pointed tips, long (0.5 to 0.75 inch) leaf stalks, and glands near the base of the leaf or along the leafstalk. Leaves are shiny, dark green above and whitish beneath. Leaf margins are mostly serrated, but will occasionally have smooth edges. Twigs are both yellow and red. It can grow to be 50 feet (16 m) tall. Shining willow is seen along both slopes up to 8,000 feet.

Goodding's black willow (*S. gooddingii*) is the only willow in the Sierra with narrow, hairless leaves that are green on both sides. Its yellowish twigs snap off neatly when pulled. Black willow can grow to be 20 to 45 feet tall, and is found mostly below 3,000 feet on the west slope.

Red willow (*S. laevigata*) is similar to shining willow, but lacks the glands on the leaf and leafstalk. The leafstalk is usually less than half an inch long. The twigs are often reddish. Growing to 25 feet tall, red willow is found along watercourses on the western slope up to 5,000 feet.

Bitter Cherry

Prunus emarginata

HABITAT & RANGE
   Throughout the Sierra along meadow edges, on damp slopes, in canyons, at streamsides, and often forming thickets among rock piles from 1,500 to 8,500 feet.

INFORMATION
   As the common name suggests, the fruit, bark, and leaves of this tree are intensely bitter, so much so that some mammals and birds will wait until there is little else available before feeding on them. The bitterness comes from hydrocyanic acid found in the twigs and new leaves, which acid also imparts a strong odor.
   Cherries typically have glands somewhere on their leaves; in bitter cherry they are found at its base. These glands are small, but readily found. Flowers bloom in midsummer and always seem full of pollinators. For a brief discussion of the horizontal lines present on the bark refer to the entry for water birch (page 96).

SIMILAR SPECIES
   Choke-cherry. Bitter cherry lacks the sharp-toothed leaf edges of choke-cherry.

ASSOCIATED SPECIES
   None.

DESCRIPTION
- **Size:** reaching 15 feet occasionally
- **Bark:** smooth, silvery to red-brown, with horizontal streaks
- **Leaves:** small, 1 to 3 inches long and up to 1 inch wide, with shallow serrated edges, often with 1 or 2 small glands at the base of the leaf
- **Fruit:** berries, red or black
- **Other:** distinct odor from freshly bruised twigs

Black Cottonwood

California Poplar, Western Balsam Poplar
Populus balsamifera spp. trichocarpa

HABITAT & RANGE
Locally common along streams and floodplains, mostly along the entire west slope up to 6,000 feet (although observed as high as 9,000 feet); found on the east slope to 7,000 feet.

INFORMATION
Black cottonwood prefers growing near streams, lakes, and marshes. Lack of aeration limits growth of the tree, so stagnant ponds and fine sediment deposited by flooding tend to slow development. Conversely, flooding by fast-moving water rich in oxygen speeds cottonwood growth.

Cottonwoods store large quantities of water in their wood. They are intolerant of shade and grow rapidly, often rising above the protection of surrounding trees where strong winds will break off their upper portions. Late frost frequently injures or kills trees.

Why the name cottonwood? Its flowers mature into fruits covered with soft, cottony hairs. During the summer, these hairs are carried by the wind and cover the forest floor.

SIMILAR SPECIES
Quaking aspen, Fremont cottonwood.

ASSOCIATED SPECIES
Willow, white alder.

NOTE
Narrow-leaved cottonwood (*P. angustifolia*) is the only poplar with willow-like leaves that are two to five times longer than broad. It can be distinguished from willows by the strong odor coming from its buds (primarily in the spring); willow buds are not aromatic. It can reach fifty

DESCRIPTION

- **Size:** tall tree, 30 to 120 feet (9-37 m)
- **Bark:** young bark is gray and smooth, becoming darker and furrowed with age
- **Leaves:** shiny dark green, paler beneath, 3 to 6 inches (7.5-15 cm) long (appreciably larger on younger trees), triangular, being widest at the base, edges with small serrations, leafstalks round
- **Fruit:** tiny, only 0.25 inch (0.6 cm) in diameter, found in light brown, hairy round capsules
- **Other:** large, pointed terminals buds, more than 0.5 inch long

feet (fifteen meters) tall and is found on the east slope of the Sierra south of Bishop near Lone Pine and Independence to 6,000 feet. It prefers growing along watercourses.

Cascara

Cascara Sagrada, Cascara Buckthorn
Rhamnus purshiana

HABITAT & RANGE
Found in moist places in the foothills below 5,000 feet from Placer County north.

INFORMATION
Early Spanish missionaries discovered the medicinal properties of the bark of the cascara, over five million pounds of which were gathered annually during World War II. Made into a pill, it was given to soldiers or crewmen to combat most illnesses. The Spanish name for the species translates as "holy bark."

The fruits are eaten by an assortment of wildlife including bears, raccoons, ring-tailed cats, band-tailed pigeons, and quail.

The Latin name for the species, *purshiana*, recognizes Frederick Pursh, a botanist who identified many plants from the Lewis and Clark expedition. Curiously, Pursh escaped to England with the Lewis and Clark plant collection in 1811.

SIMILAR SPECIES
White alder. Cascara has a black berry, while alder does not produce berries.

ASSOCIATED SPECIES
Found in the understory of Pacific ponderosa pine.

DESCRIPTION
- **Size:** large shrub, occasionally tree-like, up to 25 feet tall
- **Bark:** smooth, gray to brown
- **Leaves:** deciduous, thin, 3 to 6 inches long, with 10 to 15 prominent side veins that run to the edge of the finely serrated leaf margins
- **Fruit:** a black berry

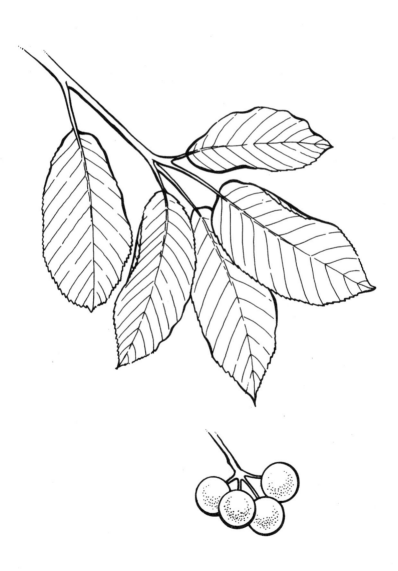

White Alder

Sierra Alder
Alnus rhombifolia

HABITAT & RANGE

Locally common in wet canyon soils usually along streams throughout the Sierra on the west slope, mostly below 5,000 feet.

INFORMATION

Cone-bearing trees are classed as coniferous, yet the white alder, which appears to bear cones, is not. The reason is that true conifers have seeds exposed on the surface of the scales while alders do not. The dangling male catkin (named for its resemblance to a cat's tail) produces a four-part flower with two to four stamens. Catkins and woody conelets can remain on the tree for up to a year. The seeds are favorites of pine siskins, grosbeaks, and finches.

Alder is not a member of the pea group, but is a nitrogen-fixer, making this essential nutrient available for other plants. The presence of alders is a more reliable indicator of running water than that of cottonwoods or willows because they generally will not grow in seasonal streams or rivers. They can tolerate spring floods rising up to three feet on their bark.

SIMILAR SPECIES

Mountain alder (*A. incana ssp.tenuifolia*) grows more as a tall shrub from Yosemite south between 4,500 and 8,000 feet on the western slope. It can be distinguished from white alder by its more serrated leaf margins, fewer side veins (white alder has nine to twelve), and by the presence of many minor veins connecting the major ones. For a comparison see the diagram on the following page.

ASSOCIATED SPECIES

Black cottonwood, willow, big-leaf maple, sycamore, Oregon ash.

DESCRIPTION

■ **Size:** medium-sized tree, 35 to 70 feet (10-22 m)

■ **Bark:** whitish to gray-brown, splitting with age

■ **Leaves:** 2 to 3.5 inches (5-9 cm) long, with 9 to 12 nearly straight, parallel veins on each side, edges are serrated

■ **Fruit:** cone, 0.4 to 0.75 inch (1-1.9 cm) long, resembling a miniature pine cone, remain closed until early spring

■ **Other:** slender, drooping flower clusters, called catkins, varying from 1 to 5 inches long, are visible throughout most of the year; also their big, brown buds are distinctive

Mountain alder

Western Choke-cherry

Common Chokecherry
Prunus virginiana

HABITAT & RANGE
   Generally found in dense thickets along streams, in clearings, and at forest edges on the western slope mostly between 2,000 and 8,000 feet.

INFORMATION
   This species is found from the Pacific Coast to the Atlantic Coast. Within this vast area minor differences in leaf and fruit shape have evolved, but the choke-cherries are all the same species. Botanist do recognize several varieties, however. The variety growing in the Sierra Nevada differs slightly from its relative in Newfoundland, and is technically known as *Prunus virginiana var. demissa*. As the common name suggests, the berries are bitter, but edible. Many birds enjoy the fruit, and choke-cherries are gathered for making jellies and jams. The immature pits and fruit contain harmful acids, but cooking removes them.

SIMILAR SPECIES
   See bitter cherry.

ASSOCIATED SPECIES
   None.

DESCRIPTION

■ **Size:** shrub-like, but will reach 20 feet on occasion

■ **Bark:** mostly smooth, gray-brown, with horizontal markings

■ **Leaves:** 2 to 5 inches long, about half as wide, with sharply serrated margins, and pointed tip; often present are 1 or 2 small glands at the base of the leafstalk

■ **Fruit:** purple berry

Water Birch

Red Birch
Betula occidentalis

HABITAT & RANGE
   Sparse in cool stream canyons on the west slope mostly south of Yosemite from 2,500 to 8,000 feet; more prevalent on the east side above the Owens Valley from 5,000 to 9,000 feet. One of the best viewing spots is along the Mt. Whitney trail.

INFORMATION
   Water birch is appropriately named because it seldom grows far from water. It generally appears as a multi-stemmed shrub, but can reach twenty-five feet tall or more. Its glossy red bark does not peel like other birches. Horizontal white lines on the bark are known as "lenticels" which aid the tree in exchanging gases necessary for photosynthesis. The long, droopy fruiting structures are called catkins, and the male catkins are thinner than the females.

SIMILAR SPECIES
   Bitter cherry and choke-cherry have similar bark, but bear fleshy fruits, feature leaves with small glands, and have twigs exuding a distinct odor.

ASSOCIATED SPECIES
   None.

DESCRIPTION

■ **Size:** shrub or small tree up to 25 feet (8 m)

■ **Bark:** smooth, shiny, red-brown, with white horizontal lines

■ **Leaves:** 1 to 2.5 inches (2.4-5 cm) long, 0.75 to 1 inch (2-2.4 cm) wide, margins saw-toothed except near the base, dark green above, pale yellow green with tiny glands beneath

■ **Fruit:** cone, 1 to 1.25 inches (2.4-3 cm) long, cylindrical, brownish

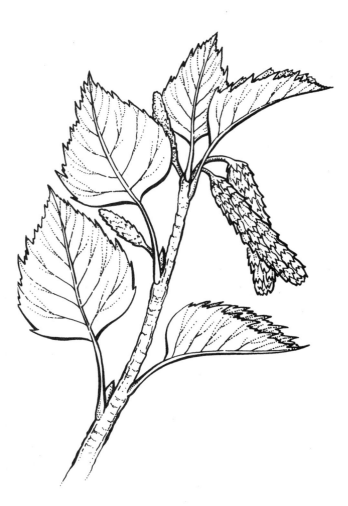

Sierra Plum

Klamath Plum, Pacific Plum
Prunus subcordata

HABITAT & RANGE
More common south of Yosemite, usually near streams or on rocky slopes between 3,000 and 6,000 feet on the western slope; common on east slope, north of Yosemite.

INFORMATION
Sierra plum is the only wild plum in the Pacific states and is easily identified when in fruit. The plums are eaten by many birds. For reasons that are unclear, trees in the southern Sierra do not seem to bear as much fruit as those growing further north. Though edible off the branch when ripe, they are tart and often used to make preserves.

In the spring the flowers appear in abundance, even before the leaves open, attracting many pollinators. Although not as common as bitter cherry and choke-cherry, Sierra plum can be observed within both Yosemite and Kings Canyon National Parks.

SIMILAR SPECIES
Bitter cherry and choke-cherry. The fruit and thorn-like twigs of Sierra plum distinguish it.

ASSOCIATED SPECIES
None.

DESCRIPTION
- **Size:** typically grows as a shrub, but will reach 15 to 20 feet under favorable conditions
- **Bark:** dark brown, cracking with age, horizontal lines evident
- **Leaves:** 1 to 3 inches long, nearly round, leaf edges sharply serrated, with glands present at the base occasionally
- **Fruit:** plum, red, about an inch long
- **Other:** thorn-like twigs diagnostic

Fremont Cottonwood

Rio Grande Cottonwood, Alamo Cottonwood
Populus fremontii ssp. fremontii

HABITAT & RANGE

Locally common along streams in the western foothills up to 2,500 feet, and in canyons on the eastern slope, mostly below 5,000 feet (occasionally observed up to 6,500 feet).

INFORMATION

Fremont cottonwood is widely distributed throughout the southwestern United States, but found only sparingly in the Sierra. It is easy to distinguish from black cottonwood because its leaves are yellowish-green on both surfaces and cannot be rolled easily between one's fingers by its stem. Black cottonwood leaves are strongly dark green above and silvery beneath, and can be easily rolled.

The tree is fast-growing and short-lived. Many individuals are shaded out by their neighbors and fall to the ground. Growing only on wet soil, it is an indicator of permanent water. It has reportedly hybridized with black cottonwood.

Fremont cottonwood was named after John C. Fremont, who discovered the species with Kit Carson near Pyramid Lake, Nevada, in January of 1844.

SIMILAR SPECIES

Aspen. Aspens grow at higher elevations, and their leaves are more circular. Black cottonwood.

ASSOCIATED SPECIES

White alder, willow.

DESCRIPTION

■ **Size:** small- to medium-sized tree, 40 to 80 feet (12-24 m)

■ **Bark:** gray, thick, deeply furrowed

■ **Leaves:** 2 to 3 inches (5-7.5 cm) long and wide, triangular, often broader than long, toothed at the margins, flattened leafstalks, same yellow-green color on both sides

■ **Fruit:** tiny, 0.5 inch (1.2 cm) long, in light-brown, egg-shaped hairless capsules

Quaking Aspen

Trembling Aspen
Populus tremuloides

HABITAT & RANGE
Locally common in many soil types, along stream borders and on damp slopes, often in pure stands, throughout the Sierra on both slopes, mostly between 6,000 and 10,000 feet.

INFORMATION
Most aspen trees are infertile with seeds lacking a viable embryo. Making things more difficult, the seeds must sprout soon after landing or they will never grow. The west's dry weather also limits reproduction by seed; most aspens reproduce through root sprouting. This clonal behavior allows aspens to cover entire hillsides and live for centuries. Clones are genetically alike as they arise from a common rootstock.

Aspens are shade-intolerant and prefer growing at forest edges and along streams. They are short-lived, usually dying at about sixty years of age. The twigs and foliage are browsed by deer, and beavers relish the bark, foliage, and buds. Many birds nest in aspen groves on the east side of the Sierra.

SIMILAR SPECIES
Cottonwood. Black cottonwood has large buds, more than half an inch, and rounded leafstalks. Aspens have smaller buds, less than half an inch, and flattened leafstalks (that are difficult to twirl between the fingers). Fremont cottonwood has larger and less serrated leaf margins, and thicker and more furrowed bark.

ASSOCIATED SPECIES
Jeffrey and lodgepole pine.

DESCRIPTION

- **Size:** small- to medium-sized tree, 10 to 65 feet (3-20 m)
- **Bark:** young bark is smooth, chalky white to yellow-green, becoming darker and more furrowed with time
- **Leaves:** nearly round, 1.25 to 3 inches (4-7.5 cm) long, with margins finely serrated, leafstalk slender and flat
- **Fruit:** tiny, light green capsules, 0.25 inch (0.6 cm) long, in drooping catkins up to 4 inches (10 cm)

Western Redbud

Judas-tree, California Redbud
Cercis occidentalis

HABITAT & RANGE
Common on the west slope throughout the Sierra mostly below 3,500 feet.

INFORMATION
Redbud is a colorful favorite of flower watchers. The trees bloom in late spring, usually at the end of April or early in May. The "red buds" unfold, unveiling a delicate purplish-pink flower. Upon close inspection, they resemble the flowers of the pea. It is not uncommon to find many pollinators around the flowers during the spring.

The wood was used by Southern Sierra Miwok Indians for making bows. Mule deer browse on the foliage.

SIMILAR SPECIES
None.

ASSOCIATED SPECIES
Interior live oak, blue oak, gray pine.

DESCRIPTION

- **Size:** more shrub-like, with multiple stems, but may reach 20 feet
- **Bark:** grayish, thin, becoming fissured with age
- **Leaves:** nearly round, to heart-shaped, with 7 to 9 main veins meeting at the notched base, 2 to 5 inches long
- **Fruit:** a brown to purple pea pod, 2 to 4 inches long

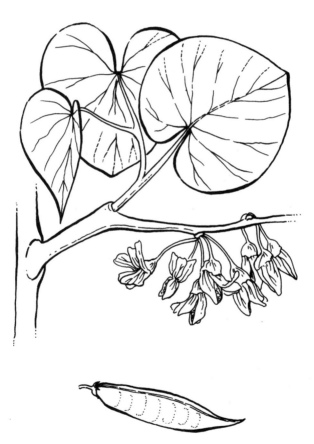

Mountain Dogwood

Flowering Dogwood, Pacific Dogwood
Cornus nuttallii

HABITAT & RANGE
Common throughout the Sierra on moist soils in wooded areas of the western slope from 2,500 to 6,000 feet.

INFORMATION
This attractive tree is unusual in that it prefers growing beneath a canopy of large conifers, such as sugar pine and sequoia. It is able to thrive in areas where most other hardwoods would fail because it can carry out photosynthesis at low light levels.

Almost everyone recognizes this species by its large white flowers, which botanists call "blooms." Each large, showy bloom is made up of many small individual flowers with yellow-green petals. Each small flower contains all the typical flower parts, such as stamens and pistils.

The red berries that appear in the fall are a preferred food of band-tailed pigeons and robins.

SIMILAR SPECIES
American and western dogwood (see below).

ASSOCIATED SPECIES
Incense cedar, Pacific ponderosa pine, sugar pine, white fir.

NOTE
In the Sierra, American dogwood (*Cornus sericea ssp. sericea*) and western dogwood (*Cornus sericea ssp. occidentalis*) are shrubby species often called "creek dogwoods," distinctly different from the mountain dogwood. Although their leaves are similar, the overall shape, size, and large "white" flowers of mountain dogwood are enough to

DESCRIPTION

- **Size:** medium-sized tree, up to 50 feet (15 m)
- **Bark:** smooth, gray to reddish-brown (occasionally scaly)
- **Leaves:** 2.5 to 4.5 inches (6-11 cm), elliptical, with 5 to 6 long, curved veins on each side of the middle vein, shiny green above, paler beneath
- **Fruit:** shiny red or orange, 0.5 inch (1.2 cm) in diameter, that grow clustered together into a dense head 1.5 inches (4 cm) across
- **Other:** notice how the branches grow in whorls around the trunk

separate it from the creek dogwoods which reach only 15 feet tall, and have smaller flowers.

American dogwood has bright red twigs (occasionally green) and moderately hairy leaves. Western dogwood lacks the bright red twigs and its leaves have more hair on the undersurface than American dogwood. Both species inhabit streamside habitats mostly between 4,000 and 8,000 feet on both slopes of the central and southern Sierra.

Pacific Madrone

Madrono, Madrone
Arbutus menziesii

HABITAT & RANGE
Common locally on the western slope below 5,000 feet mostly north of Yosemite.

DESCRIPTION
The smooth, red, or brown peeling bark is unique among Sierran trees. Manzanita, a shrub and also a member of the heath family, has similar bark and flowers (urn-shaped), but its leaves are smaller (1.5 to 2 inches) and rounder. Other related heaths include blueberries, huckleberries and cranberries.

The fruits of the madrone are eaten by many animals, including deer, ringtails, band-tailed pigeons, waxwings, quail, and songbird species. The madrone can live as long as two hundred years.

Archibald Menzies was a Scottish botanist who collected the first specimens of many western trees, including madrone. His name appears as part of the scientific name of many of these species.

SIMILAR SPECIES
None.

ASSOCIATED SPECIES
None.

DESCRIPTION
■ **Size:** medium-sized tree between 20 and 60 feet (6-18 m)
■ **Bark:** smooth, red, outer bark will peel away revealing a yellow or gray inner layer
■ **Leaves:** evergreen, thick, 2.5 to 5.5 inches long, with prominent veins, and slightly wavy margins (especially on younger trees)
■ **Fruit:** fleshy, red berry

California Bay

California Laurel, Oregon-myrtle, Pepperwood
Umbellularia californica

HABITAT & RANGE
Common on moist soils in mountain canyons and valleys throughout the Sierra up to 5,500 feet.

INFORMATION
This tree's many common names are confusing to those who are not familiar with them. The umbrella-like flowers are responsible for its generic name, *Umbellularia*.

When crushed, the foliage, twigs and other parts are strongly aromatic. Vapor (camphor-like) from the leaves can cause sneezing, headache, sinus irritation, and other discomforts. Most people, however, have no reaction.

Stellar's jays and small rodents eat the fruits. All parts of the tree have served human needs; California Indians used California bay saplings for bows and consumed its nuts by grinding them into meal for small cakes, while trappers made a tea from the leaves as a cure for stomach ailments and headaches. Today, the leaves are used to provide flavor for soups and stews.

SIMILAR SPECIES
None.

ASSOCIATED SPECIES
See "Ponderosa Pine/Mixed Coniferous Belt" on page 114.

DESCRIPTION

- **Size:** medium-sized tree 40 to 80 feet (12-24 m)
- **Bark:** thin, green to reddish brown
- **Leaves:** evergreen, shiny dark green above, dull and paler beneath, 2 to 5 inches (5-13 cm) long, 0.5 to 1.5 inches (1.2-4 cm) wide, slender, thick and leathery, and aromatic when crushed
- **Fruit:** berry-like, greenish-purple 0.75 to 1 inch (2-2.5 cm) long, enclosing a large brown seed

Curl-leaf Mountain-Mahogany

Curlleaf Cercocarpus
Cercocarpus ledifolius

HABITAT & RANGE
Common on dry, rocky mountain slopes from 4,000 to 10,500 feet on eastern slopes throughout the Sierra.

INFORMATION
Mountain-mahoganies are large shrubs or small trees found only in the United States and Mexico. They are members of the rose family and are not related to the neo-tropical mahogany (*Swietenia*) associated with valuable cabinet wood.

Highly drought-resistant and usually restricted to rocky, arid slopes and ridges, mountain-mahogany appears to be able to counteract the sterility of the soil by making its own supply of nitrates with the help of bacteria found in its root nodules.

It is browsed by deer and sheep. The name mahogany may come from the reddish brown wood, which is so dense that a freshly cut piece will sink if placed in water. For a discussion of the unique hairy seed see the entry for birch-leaf mountain-mahogany.

SIMILAR SPECIES
None.

ASSOCIATED SPECIES
Singleleaf pinyon pine.

DESCRIPTION

- **Size:** large shrub or small tree, 15 to 30 feet (4.5-9 m)
- **Bark:** reddish-brown, thick, becoming furrowed with age
- **Leaves:** evergreen, small and slender, 0.5 to 1.25 inches (1.2-3 cm), less than 0.5 inch (1 cm) wide, with leaf edges that curl under
- **Fruit:** tiny, 0.25 inch (0.6 cm), but featuring a conspicuous, long, whitish, hairy, twisted tail, 1.5 to 3 inches (4-7.5 cm)

APPENDIX A.

DOMINANT TREES FOUND IN ELEVATIONAL BELTS

Ponderosa Pine / Mixed Coniferous Belt
(3-4,000 to 6-7,000 feet)

Pacific Ponderosa and Sugar Pine, Incense Cedar, White Fir, Douglas-fir, Giant Sequoia, Canyon Live Oak, California Black Oak, Big-leaf Maple, Mountain Dogwood, Black Cottonwood, California Bay

Foothill Belt
(500 to 3-4,500 feet)

Gray and Knobcone Pines, California Nutmeg Blue Oak, Interior Live Oak, California Buckeye, Redbud

Great Central Valley
(up to 500 feet)

White Oak, Western Sycamore, Fremont Cottonwood

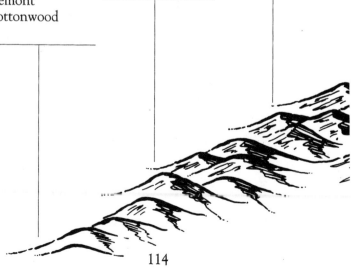

114

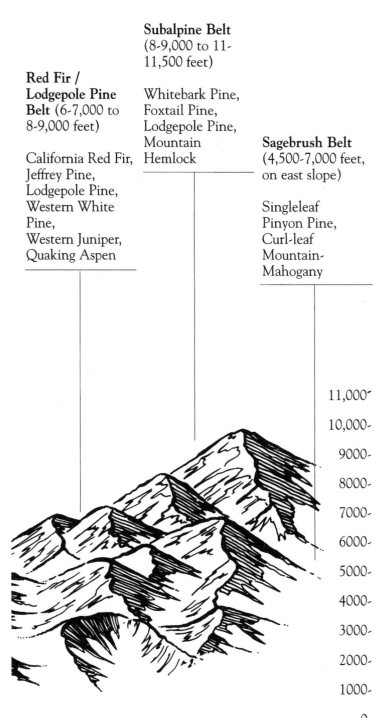

Subalpine Belt
(8-9,000 to 11-11,500 feet)

Whitebark Pine,
Foxtail Pine,
Lodgepole Pine,
Mountain
Hemlock

**Red Fir /
Lodgepole Pine
Belt** (6-7,000 to
8-9,000 feet)

California Red Fir,
Jeffrey Pine,
Lodgepole Pine,
Western White
Pine,
Western Juniper,
Quaking Aspen

Sagebrush Belt
(4,500-7,000 feet,
on east slope)

Singleleaf
Pinyon Pine,
Curl-leaf
Mountain-
Mahogany

11,000-
10,000-
9000-
8000-
7000-
6000-
5000-
4000-
3000-
2000-
1000-
0-
Elevation in feet

115

APPENDIX B.

LIST OF SOME COMMON NON-NATIVE TREES AROUND SIERRA SETTLEMENT

Acacia
Apple (*Malus* sp.)
Black Locust (*Robinia pseudoacacia*)
California Black Walnut (*Juglans californica*)
Deodar Cedar (*Cedrus deodara*)
Lombardy Poplar (*Populus nigra*)
Sweet Gum (*Liquidambar* sp.)
Tree of Heaven (*Ailanthus altissima*)

APPENDIX C.

PONDEROSA AND JEFFREY PINES COMPARED

These trees are easily confused, but with practice and patience you should be able to distinguish them. Focus on the characteristics at right, paying particular attention to the more reliable traits (marked with an asterisk).

	PACIFIC PONDEROSA PINE	JEFFREY PINE
Cones		
*Size:	3 to 5 inches	5 to 8 inches
*Density:	light	heavy
Scales with spines that:	turn outward	turn inward
Shading of spines:	upper surface lighter than lower one	no distinction
Scales:	moderately flexible	rigid
Mature Bark		
*Scales of inner surface:	yellowish, soft, with small dark resin pits	pinkish, hard, with no resin pits
Odor:	absent to faint resinous	strong butterscotch or vanilla
Color:	light yellowish tan	dark red, to red or brown
Fissures:	well-separated, shallow	close together, deep
Terminal Buds		
At base:	often sticky	not sticky
New Twigs		
Outer branch thickness:	like a pencil	slightly greater than a pencil
Needles		
Color	yellow-green	dull blue-green
Foliage	less dense	more dense
Elevations	3,000 to 7,000 feet	5,200 to 9,500 feet

APPENDIX D.

PLANT RELATIONSHIPS

Although having prior knowledge of plant taxonomy may not benefit your field identification, it will enhance your understanding of the relationships that exist between plants as well as deepen your appreciation for the diversity of life on earth.

KINGDOM Plantae

Division Pinophyta (Cone-producers)

Class Pinopsida

Family Taxaceae
>Taxus (Yew)
>Torreya (California Nutmeg)

Family Pinaceae
>Abies (Fir)
>Pinus (Pines)
>Pseudotsuga (Douglas-fir)
>Tsuga (Hemlock)

Family Taxodiaceae
>Sequoiadendron (Sequoia)

Family Cupressaceae
>Calocedrus (Incense Cedar)
>Juniperus (Juniper)

Division Magnoliophyta (Flower-producers)

Class Magnoliopsida

Family Lauraceae
>Umbellularia (California Bay)

Family Platanaceae
      Platanus (Sycamore)
Family Fagacae
      Quercus (Oaks)
Family Betulaceae
      Alnus (Alder)
      Betula (Water Birch)
Family Salicaceae
      Populus (Cottonwood)
      Salix (Willow)
Family Ericaceae
      Arbutus (Madrone)
Family Rosaceae
      Cercocarpus (Mountain-Mahoganies)
      Prunus (Cherries)
Family Cornaceae
      Cornus (Dogwood)
Family Rhamnaceae
      Rhamnus (Buckthorn)
Family Staphyleaceae
      Staphylea (Bladdernut)
Family Aceraceae
      Acer (Maple)

REFERENCES

Arno, Stephen F. *Discovering Sierra Trees*. Yosemite N.P.: Yosemite Association and Sequoia Natural History Association, 1973.

Arno, Stephen F. *Timberline: Mountain and Arctic Forest Frontiers*. Seattle: The Mountaineers, 1984.

Brockman, C. Frank. *Trees of North America*. New York: Western Publishing Co., 1986.

Cole, James E. *Cone-Bearing Trees of Yosemite National Park*. Yosemite N.P.: Yosemite Natural History Association, 1963.

Griggs, Tom. "Valley Oaks: Can They Be Saved?" *Fremontia* 18 (July 1990): 48-51.

Harvey, H. Thomas. *The Sequoias of Yosemite National Park*. Yosemite N.P: Yosemite Association, 1978.

Hickman, James C., ed. *The Jepson Manual, Higher Plants of California*. Berkeley: University of California Press, 1993.

Lanner, Ronald M. *The Piñon Pine: A Natural & Cultural History*. Reno: University of Nevada Press, 1980.

Little, Elbert L. *The Audubon Society Field Guide to North American Trees (Western Region)*. New York: Alfred A. Knopf, 1980.

McMinn, Howard E. *An Illustrated Manual of California Shrubs*. Berkeley: University of California Press, 1951.

Mensing, Scott. "Blue Oak Regeneration in the Tehachapi Mountains." *Fremontia* 18 (July 1990): 38-41.

Munz, Philip A. *A California Flora*. Berkeley: University of California Press, 1959.

Pavlik, Bruce M. *Oaks of California*. Santa Barbara: Cachuma Press, 1991.

Peattie, Donald C. *A Natural History of Western Trees*. Boston: Houghton Mifflin Co., 1953.

Petrides, George and Olivia. *Western Trees*. Boston: Houghton Mifflin Co., 1992.

Storer, Tracy I., and Robert L. Usinger. *Sierra Nevada Natural History*. Berkeley: University of California Press, 1963.

Sudworth, George B. *Forest Trees of the Pacific Slope*. New York: Dover Publications, 1967.

Thomas, John H., and Dennis R. Parnell. *Native Shrubs of the Sierra Nevada*. Berkeley: University of California Press, 1974.

U.S. Forest Service. *Silvics of Forest Trees of the United States*. Agriculture Handbook 271. Washington, D.C.: U.S. Government Printing Office, 1965.

Weeden, Norman F. *A Sierra Nevada Flora*. Berkeley: Wilderness Press, 1996.

Whitman, Ann H. *Familiar Trees of North America - Western Region*. New York: Alfred A. Knopf, 1986.

Whitney, Stephen. *Western Forests*. New York: Alfred A. Knopf, 1985.

INDEX

Page numbers in bold indicate the primary reference for the entry.

YOSEMITE CONSERVANCY.

Providing For Yosemite's Future

Through the support of donors, Yosemite Conservancy provides grants and support to Yosemite National Park to help preserve and protect Yosemite today and for future generations. The work funded by Yosemite Conservancy is visible throughout the park, from trail rehabilitation to wildlife protection and habitat restoration. The Conservancy is dedicated to enhancing the visitor experience and providing a deeper connection to the park through outdoor programs, volunteering and wilderness services. Thanks to dedicated supporters, the Conservancy has provided more than $81 million in grants to Yosemite National Park.

yosemiteconservancy.org